# COOKING
### WITH
# REGIS & KATHIE LEE

# COOKING
## WITH
# REGIS & KATHIE LEE

REGIS PHILBIN & KATHIE LEE GIFFORD

WITH
BARBARA ALBRIGHT

HYPERION                    NEW YORK

Editorial production: SPECTRUM AMERICA, New York
Design: MICHAELIS/CARPELIS, New York

Text Copyright © 1993 Regis Philbin and Lambchop Productions, Ltd.

For information, address inquiries to: HYPERION, 114 Fifth Avenue, New York, New York 10011

FIRST EDITION
10  9  8  7  6  5  4  3  2

# CONTENTS

A Word from Regis & Kathie Lee ......................... *xi*

Introduction: Behind the Scenes at "Live" ................. *xiii*

**CHAPTER 1:** *Let's Start the Show* ...................... *1*
   *Super Bowl Salsa* ................................... *3*
   *Hard Rock "Guac"* .................................. *4*
   *Swiss Cheese Fondue* ............................... *6*
   *Buffalo Chicken Wings* ............................. *7*
   *Nautical Nuggets* .................................. *8*
   *Vegetable Egg Rolls* ............................... *10*
   *Robin Leach's Mediterranean Eggplant Pie* .................. *12*
   *Sesame Bay Scallops* ............................... *13*
   *Chef Tell's Fast and Fabulous Hors D'oeuvres* ............... *14*

**CHAPTER 2:** *Soup's On* .............................. *17*
   *Clever Lettuce Soup* ............................... *19*
   *Sensational Chicken Soup* .......................... *20*
   *Down-Home Split Pea Soup* ......................... *21*
   *Bowl of the Wife of Kit Carson* ........................ *22*
   *New England Clam Chowder* ......................... *23*
   *Super Bowl Chili* .................................. *25*
   *Phyllis Diller's Oyster Stew* ....................... *27*
   *Vegetable Soup* .................................... *28*
   *Hearty Red Lentil Lemon Soup* ....................... *29*

**CHAPTER 3:** *Pasta Possibilities* ...................... *31*
   *Papardelle with Sausage* ........................... *33*
   *Linguine with Sweet Red Pepper Sauce* .................... *34*
   *Pasta with Crawfish, Shrimp, or Crabmeat in Cream Sauce* ...... *36*
   *Bat-Wing Pasta* ................................... *37*

Santa Fe Chili Pasta .................................... 38
Party Pasta Salad ..................................... 40
Linda Dano's Marinara Sauce .......................... 41
Pasta con Amore ...................................... 42
Farfalle à la Marcello .................................. 43
Pasta with Broccoli and Mushrooms ..................... 44
Penne Pasta with Prosciutto Sauce ...................... 45
Bucatine Cacio e Pepe ................................. 46
James Darren's Grandmom's Pasta ...................... 47

**CHAPTER 4: *Mostly Meat*** ............................. 49
Steak Lorenzo ........................................ 51
Blackened Steak ...................................... 52
Traditional Marinated Steak Barbecue ................... 54
Flaming Fajitas ....................................... 56
Steak Diane with Cognac ............................... 58
Clever Pizzaiola Meatballs ............................. 59
Tacos à la Mayor ..................................... 60
The Governor's Loaf .................................. 61
Mom Kaufman's Meatloaf .............................. 62
Rusty-Burgers ........................................ 63
Classic New England Pot Roast ......................... 64
Jack Daniel's Rib Glaze ............................... 66
Barbecue Ribs Excalibur ............................... 67
Roast Pork with Apricots .............................. 69
Pork Tenderloin Medallions with Green Peppercorn Sauce ........ 70
Gypsy Cutlets ........................................ 71
Stuffed Pork Chops with Apple Butter .................... 72
Lamb Chops in Parmesan Crust ......................... 74
Lamb Chops with Cracked Pepper and Tarragon .......... 75
Shepherd's Pie ....................................... 76
Lamb Paprikas ....................................... 78
Navarin of Lamb ..................................... 79
Veal Parmigiana ..................................... 80
Veal Casino ......................................... 82
Veal Birds .......................................... 83

**CHAPTER 5: *Fowl Play*** ............................... 85
Moghlai Chicken ..................................... 87
Yogurt Chicken ...................................... 88
Caribbean-Fried Chicken .............................. 89

Roasted Chili Chicken . . . . . . . . . . . . . . . . . . . . . . . . . . . . . . . . 90
Bastille Day Chicken . . . . . . . . . . . . . . . . . . . . . . . . . . . . . . . . . 92
Chicken Bundles of Love . . . . . . . . . . . . . . . . . . . . . . . . . . . . . . 93
Chicken with Prosciutto and Cheese with Mushroom Sauce . . . . . . . . 94
Breast of Chicken with Garden Vegetables . . . . . . . . . . . . . . . . . . . 96
Chicken Pilaf . . . . . . . . . . . . . . . . . . . . . . . . . . . . . . . . . . . . . 97
Southwestern Pan-Fried Chicken . . . . . . . . . . . . . . . . . . . . . . . . . 98
Matzoh Balls with Chicken . . . . . . . . . . . . . . . . . . . . . . . . . . . . . 99
Baked Chicken with Pastry . . . . . . . . . . . . . . . . . . . . . . . . . . . . 101
Turkey Pot Pie . . . . . . . . . . . . . . . . . . . . . . . . . . . . . . . . . . . 102
Grilled Chicken with Watermelon Pico de Gallo . . . . . . . . . . . . . . 104
Grilled Chicken with Fruit . . . . . . . . . . . . . . . . . . . . . . . . . . . . 105
Jamaican Jerk Rub . . . . . . . . . . . . . . . . . . . . . . . . . . . . . . . . . 106
Prehistoric Barbecued Chicken . . . . . . . . . . . . . . . . . . . . . . . . . 107
Chicken Pickup Sticks . . . . . . . . . . . . . . . . . . . . . . . . . . . . . . . 109

**CHAPTER 6:** *Under the Sea* . . . . . . . . . . . . . . . . . . . . . . . . . . . 111
Shrimp Samantha with Andouille . . . . . . . . . . . . . . . . . . . . . . . . 113
Grilled Shrimp Salad with Ginger . . . . . . . . . . . . . . . . . . . . . . . . 114
Grandma Cecilia's "Shrimp on Fire" . . . . . . . . . . . . . . . . . . . . . . 115
Bay State Wiggle . . . . . . . . . . . . . . . . . . . . . . . . . . . . . . . . . . 116
Ginger Shrimp . . . . . . . . . . . . . . . . . . . . . . . . . . . . . . . . . . . 118
Scallops with Tomato Saffron Sauce . . . . . . . . . . . . . . . . . . . . . . 119
Smoked Oriental Seafood . . . . . . . . . . . . . . . . . . . . . . . . . . . . 120
Lemon Crumb-Baked Cod . . . . . . . . . . . . . . . . . . . . . . . . . . . . 121
Seasoned Rice Seafood Salad . . . . . . . . . . . . . . . . . . . . . . . . . . 122
Irish Salmon with Cucumber Sauce . . . . . . . . . . . . . . . . . . . . . . 124
Salmon with Avocado Sauce . . . . . . . . . . . . . . . . . . . . . . . . . . . 126
Pan-Seared Salmon with Zucchini, Spinach, and Broccoli . . . . . . . . 127
Warm Tuna Salad . . . . . . . . . . . . . . . . . . . . . . . . . . . . . . . . . 129
Beer Batter Fish and Spicy Dipping Sauce . . . . . . . . . . . . . . . . . . 130
Fish with Puff Sauce . . . . . . . . . . . . . . . . . . . . . . . . . . . . . . . 131
Salmon Fillets with Crispy Skin . . . . . . . . . . . . . . . . . . . . . . . . . 133
Seafood Shish Kebab . . . . . . . . . . . . . . . . . . . . . . . . . . . . . . . 134
Lola's Quick Red Snapper . . . . . . . . . . . . . . . . . . . . . . . . . . . . 135
Santa Barbara Surfer's Sauté . . . . . . . . . . . . . . . . . . . . . . . . . . 136
Snapper Caprice . . . . . . . . . . . . . . . . . . . . . . . . . . . . . . . . . . 138

**CHAPTER 7:** *On the Side* . . . . . . . . . . . . . . . . . . . . . . . . . . . . 139
Perfect Southwestern Potato Salad . . . . . . . . . . . . . . . . . . . . . . . 141
Killer Mashed Potatoes . . . . . . . . . . . . . . . . . . . . . . . . . . . . . . 142

Spoon Bread . . . . . . . . . . . . . . . . . . . . . . . . . . . . . . . . . . 143
Garlic Rice with Pine Nuts . . . . . . . . . . . . . . . . . . . . . . . 144
Riverbank Barbecue Baked Beans . . . . . . . . . . . . . . . . . 145
Perfect Corn on the Cob . . . . . . . . . . . . . . . . . . . . . . . . 146
Corn Fritters . . . . . . . . . . . . . . . . . . . . . . . . . . . . . . . . . 147
Clever Cleaver Sweet Spring Salad . . . . . . . . . . . . . . . . 148
Wild Mushrooms with Garlic and Olive Oil . . . . . . . . . . . 149
Noodle Pudding . . . . . . . . . . . . . . . . . . . . . . . . . . . . . . . 150
Traditional Italian Bread . . . . . . . . . . . . . . . . . . . . . . . . 152
Irish Freckle Bread . . . . . . . . . . . . . . . . . . . . . . . . . . . . 153

CHAPTER 8: Rise & Shine! . . . . . . . . . . . . . . . . . . . . . . 155
Bing Cherry Crumb Cake . . . . . . . . . . . . . . . . . . . . . . . 157
Honey-Nut Apple Muffins . . . . . . . . . . . . . . . . . . . . . . . 159
Blueberry Oat Muffins . . . . . . . . . . . . . . . . . . . . . . . . . 161
Mother's Day Turnover . . . . . . . . . . . . . . . . . . . . . . . . . 163
Easy French Crêpes . . . . . . . . . . . . . . . . . . . . . . . . . . . . 164
Sweetheart Frittata . . . . . . . . . . . . . . . . . . . . . . . . . . . . 165
Quiche . . . . . . . . . . . . . . . . . . . . . . . . . . . . . . . . . . . . . . 166
Cocoa Waffles . . . . . . . . . . . . . . . . . . . . . . . . . . . . . . . . 167

CHAPTER 9: On the Lighter Side . . . . . . . . . . . . . . . . . 169
Spiced Apple Napoleon . . . . . . . . . . . . . . . . . . . . . . . . . 171
Saffron Apples with Frozen Pistachio Yogurt . . . . . . . . . 172
Persimmon and Maple Fool . . . . . . . . . . . . . . . . . . . . . . 174
Shrimp and Vegetables . . . . . . . . . . . . . . . . . . . . . . . . . 175
Tucson Chicken . . . . . . . . . . . . . . . . . . . . . . . . . . . . . . . 176
Texas-Style Chicken or Beef Skillet . . . . . . . . . . . . . . . . 177
Jo Jo's Juicy Shrimp . . . . . . . . . . . . . . . . . . . . . . . . . . . 178
Potato Latkes . . . . . . . . . . . . . . . . . . . . . . . . . . . . . . . . 180
Chocolate Love Bites . . . . . . . . . . . . . . . . . . . . . . . . . . . 182
Low-Cal Chocolate Brownies . . . . . . . . . . . . . . . . . . . . . 183

CHAPTER 10: Grand Finales . . . . . . . . . . . . . . . . . . . . . 185
Chocolate Pecan Pie . . . . . . . . . . . . . . . . . . . . . . . . . . . 187
Chocolate Whipped Cream Pie . . . . . . . . . . . . . . . . . . . 188
Island Lime Pie . . . . . . . . . . . . . . . . . . . . . . . . . . . . . . . 189
Chef Paul Prudhomme's Indian Pudding . . . . . . . . . . . . 190
Georgia Peach Bread Pudding . . . . . . . . . . . . . . . . . . . . 192
Homemade Banana Pudding . . . . . . . . . . . . . . . . . . . . . 193
German Apple Cake . . . . . . . . . . . . . . . . . . . . . . . . . . . . 194

The Chocolate Denseness . . . . . . . . . . . . . . . . . . . . . . . . . . . . . 195
White Chocolate Cheesecake . . . . . . . . . . . . . . . . . . . . . . . . . . 198
Chocolate Oblivion Truffle Torte . . . . . . . . . . . . . . . . . . . . . . 199
Pan de Jerez (Chocolate Sherry Torte) . . . . . . . . . . . . . . . . . . 201
Aunt Pittypat's Pecan Pound Cake . . . . . . . . . . . . . . . . . . . . 203
Joseph's Knockout Carrot Cake . . . . . . . . . . . . . . . . . . . . . . 205
Chocolate Turtle Cookies . . . . . . . . . . . . . . . . . . . . . . . . . . . . 207
Merveilles . . . . . . . . . . . . . . . . . . . . . . . . . . . . . . . . . . . . . . . . . 208
Million-Dollar Fudge . . . . . . . . . . . . . . . . . . . . . . . . . . . . . . . 210

CHAPTER 11: Let's Celebrate . . . . . . . . . . . . . . . . . . . . . . . . 213
New Year's Trifle . . . . . . . . . . . . . . . . . . . . . . . . . . . . . . . . . . 215
Easter Roast Leg of Lamb with Scallions and Potatoes . . . . . . . . . 216
Gaeltach Chicken . . . . . . . . . . . . . . . . . . . . . . . . . . . . . . . . . . 217
Fighting Irish Flambé . . . . . . . . . . . . . . . . . . . . . . . . . . . . . . . 218
Thankful Rice . . . . . . . . . . . . . . . . . . . . . . . . . . . . . . . . . . . . 220
Christmas Punch . . . . . . . . . . . . . . . . . . . . . . . . . . . . . . . . . . 221
The Polar Breeze . . . . . . . . . . . . . . . . . . . . . . . . . . . . . . . . . . 222
Kentucky Christmas Ham . . . . . . . . . . . . . . . . . . . . . . . . . . . 223
Roast Christmas Goose . . . . . . . . . . . . . . . . . . . . . . . . . . . . . 224
Holiday Sweet Potato Pecan Pies . . . . . . . . . . . . . . . . . . . . . 225
Miniature Pecan Pies . . . . . . . . . . . . . . . . . . . . . . . . . . . . . . . 227
Christmas Cheesecake . . . . . . . . . . . . . . . . . . . . . . . . . . . . . . 228
Christmas Tiramisu . . . . . . . . . . . . . . . . . . . . . . . . . . . . . . . . 230

CHAPTER 12: Family Favorites . . . . . . . . . . . . . . . . . . . . . . 233
Kathie Lee's Sausage and Sage Thanksgiving Stuffing . . . . . . . . . . 235
Kathie Lee's Special Turkey Marsala . . . . . . . . . . . . . . . . . . . 236
Michie's Sweet Potato "Soufflé" . . . . . . . . . . . . . . . . . . . . . . 237
Kringa (Swedish Puff) . . . . . . . . . . . . . . . . . . . . . . . . . . . . . . 238
Jalapeño Casserole . . . . . . . . . . . . . . . . . . . . . . . . . . . . . . . . 241
Gelman's Chicken Amore . . . . . . . . . . . . . . . . . . . . . . . . . . . . 242
Joy's Pasta with Chicken and Broccoli . . . . . . . . . . . . . . . . . . 243

Resources . . . . . . . . . . . . . . . . . . . . . . . . . . . . . . . . . . . . . . . . . . 245

Index . . . . . . . . . . . . . . . . . . . . . . . . . . . . . . . . . . . . . . . . . . . . . 251

# A WORD FROM

# *R*EGIS & *K*ATHIE *L*EE

———■□■———

*S*how business is a collaborative industry, if ever there was one, and this cookbook certainly shows what collaboration is all about!

Many thanks to all the people who have generously and enthusiastically shared their recipes with us to be included in this book. We have enjoyed having them on the show, and we are delighted to have this permanent record to enable us to enjoy their delicious recipes again and again in our own homes. Our gratitude, too, to the publishers and restaurants who have given us permission to reprint recipes.

Thanks are especially due to Mary Kellogg, Carol Seminara, and Robin Shallow of Buena Vista Productions for their commitment to this cookbook. We couldn't have done it without their organized record-keeping of all the guests who have appeared on "Live" and their detective work in sleuthing out the ways and means of contacting the contributors.

Special credit also goes to Isabelle Vita, Leslie Weiner, and Lynn Albright for their careful testing to make sure that the recipes work perfectly. And thank you, Ted and Samantha Westray, for letting us borrow your wife and mother, Barbara Albright, our invaluable editor, for so long.

Of course, we can't neglect mentioning Michael Gelman, executive producer, and the producing staff: Barbara Fight, Suzy Hayman, Rosemary Kalikow, Victoria Lang, Cynthia Lockheart, David Mullen, Isabel Rivera, Delores Spruell, and Joanne Tardieu. Thanks also to Jim Griffin, our agent, for his business savvy in getting this production together in such fine style.

A very special thank-you to Leslie Wells, our editor at Hyperion, and to her extremely helpful assistant, Ellen Cowhey, for their belief in the value of a written record of the excellent recipes—representative of the best of American cooking—that have been demonstrated on "Live with Regis & Kathie Lee."

*Bon appétit!*

# INTRODUCTION:
# BEHIND THE SCENES AT "LIVE"

———◼———

*I*f you have ever been disappointed that you didn't get a recipe scribbled down, or that the VCR wasn't set correctly, and that then you never got around to sending for the newsletter, here it finally is—the permanent record of the *best* recipes featured on "Live with Regis & Kathie Lee" since the show's national syndication in September 1988.

Just like the weather, food is a topic that everyone has in common—which is why cooking demonstrations fit in so well with the vibrant, chatty nature of "Live with Regis & Kathie Lee." Ever since Regis was the host of "AM-LA," he has felt that food is an important element of talk shows. Even people who don't usually cook enjoy Regis's entertaining additions to culinary segments.

Executive Producer Michael Gelman and his staff have carefully selected the people who demonstrate recipes on the show. Given the opportunity to cook on national television, the guest chefs have chosen their very best recipes, so this could be called the ultimate community cookbook—because it features top recipes from the very special community of food experts who have appeared on "Live."

When asked how the guests and recipes for food segments are decided on, Gelman (as Regis affectionately calls him) says that he and the producers are always looking at what is happening in the food world. Sometimes a unique or popular book will be the reason for choosing a recipe demonstrator or a particular recipe. Hot, new, "happening" restaurant chefs are constantly featured, as are celebrities who cook as a hobby.

The producers have to consider balance in the food segments. Usually, they try to include cuisine that is healthful, but they also know that people don't always want to eat with only nutrition in mind. Recipes are often selected because they are appropriate to a season or a special holiday. Of course, any input from Regis and Kathie Lee always gets top consideration. Because each of them dines out frequently—at least five times a week—they know which restaurants in the New York area offer the best food.

The show always tries to feature dishes that people would actually cook at home—maybe just a basic recipe with an out-of-the-ordinary twist to it. If a recipe calls for an expensive or hard-to-find ingredient, the recipe creator is always asked for a substitute that is less expensive or more readily available. While the hosts and guests have fun with the recipe on the air, the producers' ultimate goal is that the viewers will want and be able to prepare the food themselves. Considering the quality and variety of recipes featured on the show, it's not surprising that Gelman loves food and takes a personal interest in each food segment. In fact, he's quite a chef himself.

While viewers only see 1½ to 10 minutes of a cooking demonstration, a lot of time goes into preparing for the segment. Because so many well-qualified people want to demonstrate recipes on "Live," it is easy for the producers to make advance arrangements for appearances. Occasionally, a segment of the show will get cancelled the day before, and a cooking segment is often a logical fill-in.

Gelman oversees four to five producers, who are in charge of making sure that each segment runs smoothly. The guest chef and producer discuss the recipe to be prepared, as well as anything special that might add extra interest to the segment. If the chef is preparing a barbecue recipe, for example, they may plan to cook on a grill on the sidewalk in front of the studio; for a dish with a Caribbean theme, they might bring in a steel-drum player and add a tropical touch to the set décor.

Prior to the show, the guest chef has to make careful plans so that everything is as organized as possible—by their very nature, both Regis and television add disorder! In addition to having *all* the equipment and ingredients on hand for the demonstration, they must give Regis a finished recipe to taste at the end of the cooking segment. Out-of-town guests often have to beg a hotel or a friend for permission to use their kitchen to ensure that Regis gets a freshly made sample of a recipe. If there are any parts of the recipe that need to be assembled ahead of time, the guest also must plan to have the complete and correct amount of ingredients.

On the day of the show, the recipe demonstrators usually arrive at the WABC studio on 67th Street and Columbus Avenue in New York City at about 7 A.M., loaded down with bags and boxes of food and equipment. As television kitchens go, the set of "Live" is very well stocked. During the excitement of "the television experience," however, things are occasionally misplaced—and woe to the cook who expects to use the blender, only to find out that the cook from an earlier segment has mistakenly packed "Live's" blender container in his bags! There is a fantastic crew at

"Live" who will run out in search of any last-minute items, and New York is renowned as a city that never sleeps, but seasoned television cooks know that it is better to come with *everything* and to have as much as possible done ahead of time.

Early on the day of the show, the producer in charge of the segment will rehearse the cooking demonstration with the guest and they may tape a short promotional piece called a "tease." While looking neat and tidy usually doesn't go hand-in-hand with food preparation, guests on "Live" benefit from the skilled attentions of the staff hairdresser and makeup expert, which helps bolster their confidence for their live appearance on national television. Then each is fitted with a microphone—and stands ready to show 18 million viewers how to cook.

Because of the show's commitment to demonstrating recipes that people will be able to re-create at home, there is a set formula for the way that recipes are demonstrated on "Live." The recipe ingredients are carefully arranged on the counter in the stage kitchen in the order that they are to be used. On the counter behind each ingredient, a small piece of paper is taped listing the quantity of the ingredient, just in case a guest has stage jitters and forgets. Before the recipe is prepared, the viewer is shown a close-up of each ingredient along with a written description.

From that point on, chefs have the challenge of getting the host (usually Regis) to help them prepare the recipe in whatever time they have to work with. Usually a crew member, stationed beside the camera, monitors the time and starts giving hand signals if Regis and the chef need to speed things up.

At the end of the segment, Regis and Kathie Lee sample the finished recipe the chef has prepared in advance. Kathie Lee insists that nothing has ever tasted horrible, but admits that some recipes are better than others. Regis says that usually the food is very good because the chefs are preparing their best dishes. In fact, Regis has often been so impressed with featured recipes that when he visits the restaurant of a guest chef, he will order a dish that was cooked on "Live." He commented that he didn't exactly know why, but he often didn't think the food tasted as good later in the day as when he sampled it on the show—maybe he is hungrier at 9:30 A.M., the food is fresher, or the recipe was prepared in smaller quantity and more precisely? Or perhaps the magic of television makes every performer (and even a plate of food) a star?

When the camera turns away from the stage kitchen to capture the next "Live" segment, there is plenty of food remaining on the counter. Ravenous crew members, who have been on duty since early morning, devour the leftovers in a free-for-all, thoughtfully saving portions for staff members who are located farther from the action.

Then the guest chef packs up the dirty dishes and leaves the set with that special aura of having been on national television—"Live with Regis & Kathie Lee."

# Let's Start the Show

# SUPER BOWL SALSA (A.K.A. THE WORLD'S GREATEST SALSA)

Francis Anthony, the Love Chef, is a frequent guest on "Live." In the early 1970s, Francis started cooking classes for beginners called "Cooking with Love." He selected that name because when his parents cooked, they always cooked with love. One of his students said that if he cooked with love, he must be the Love Chef. The name stuck—and that's how we know and love him today! On Super Bowl Sunday, serve this salsa with your favorite "dippers," such as taco chips and miniature pita breads.

1    can (28 ounces) whole peeled tomatoes and juice, chopped
3    cups thinly sliced celery
1    can (19 ounces) chick peas, pureed
1    medium cucumber, peeled, seeded, and diced
1    cup chopped fresh cilantro
½    cup finely chopped scallions
1    can (4 ounces) chopped green chilies
2    tablespoons freshly squeezed lime juice
1    tablespoon vinegar
1    tablespoon (or less) hot sauce
½    tablespoon granulated sugar
2    garlic cloves, finely chopped
1    teaspoon ground cumin
1    teaspoon dried oregano leaves

▪ In a large glass bowl, combine all of the ingredients. Cover and refrigerate until ready to serve. This dip is best made the day before.

*Makes about 2 quarts.*

# HARD ROCK "GUAC"

This fantastically good recipe for guacamole comes from Beany Macgregor, who at the time he appeared on "Live" was the chef of the Hard Rock Café on 57th Street in New York City. Memorabilia from the restaurant provided an appropriate setting for this Hard Rock recipe, and Regis entered into the spirit of the segment by wearing the purple jacket Prince had worn on the album "Purple Rain." In his enthusiasm, he broke a guitar string, which Beany threatened to make him pay for. Beany is now the corporate executive chef of Hard Rock Café International. In the box, he suggests some uses for leftover guacamole.

| | |
|---|---|
| 6 | ripe Hass avocados, pitted and peeled |
| 1½ | cups seeded and chopped tomatoes |
| 1 | small Spanish onion, chopped |
| 1 | tablespoon freshly squeezed lemon or lime juice |
| 1 | tablespoon salt |
| 1 | teaspoon Worcestershire sauce |
| 2 | teaspoons Tabasco |
| 1 | teaspoon cayenne pepper |
| ¾ | teaspoon garlic powder or finely chopped fresh garlic |
| ¾ | teaspoon ground cumin |
| | Tortilla chips and raw vegetables, for serving with the guacamole |
| | Salsa |

▪ Place the avocados in a large bowl and use a large spoon to break them up. Add the remaining ingredients except the chips and raw vegetables. Using a spoon, stir everything together, taking care to leave it slightly chunky. Serve with the tortilla chips, raw vegetables, and a spicy salsa.

*Makes 10 to 12 appetizer servings.*

## USES FOR LEFTOVER GUACAMOLE FROM BEANY MACGREGOR

**Guacamole Mayonnaise:** Combine 1 cup of mayonnaise with ½ cup of pureed guacamole.

**Guacamole Vinaigrette:** Combine ¼ cup of guacamole with vinaigrette and fresh cilantro to taste.

**Guacamole Butter:** Whip ¾ pound of softened unsalted butter with ½ cup of guacamole. Add chopped cilantro, lemon juice, ground cumin, cayenne pepper, and salt to taste.

**Chicken Breast Stuffed with Guacamole Butter:** Before baking an 8-ounce boneless chicken breast, stuff it with ¼ cup of guacamole butter and spread 2 tablespoons of guacamole butter between the breast and the skin.

Steve Friedman/Buena Vista Television

*Oh, Reeege!*

# SWISS CHEESE FONDUE

For a taste of Switzerland, try the following classic from Kurt Mezger. Kurt is the chef and owner of the Chalet Swiss restaurant in Welches, Oregon, near Mount Hood. This is a great appetizer to serve as a party icebreaker because it makes everyone get involved. According to Kurt, if a lady loses her bread cube in the fondue, she owes the man on her right a kiss. If a man has such a mishap, he must buy the next round of drinks. At home, he owes his hostess a kiss.

| | |
|---|---|
| 1 | garlic clove, peeled and cut in half |
| 10 | ounces Swiss Emmental cheese, grated |
| 10 | ounces Swiss Gruyère cheese, grated |
| 4 | teaspoons cornstarch |
| 2 | cups dry white wine |
| 1 | tablespoon freshly squeezed lemon juice |
| 1¼ | ounces Kirschwasser (clear cherry brandy) |
| | Pinch of ground nutmeg |
| | Pepper to taste |
| | French or Italian bread, cut into 1-inch cubes, and/or raw vegetables (such as mushrooms, cherry tomatoes, cauliflower florets, broccoli florets, celery sticks, and carrot sticks), for dipping |

■ Rub the inside of a large heavy saucepot with the garlic clove. Discard the garlic.

■ Combine the cheeses and cornstarch in the saucepot. Stir in the wine and lemon juice. Heat the cheese mixture over high heat, stirring constantly, until the cheese is melted and creamy. Stir in the Kirschwasser, nutmeg, and pepper. Cook for 1 minute longer.

■ Transfer the fondue to a heated fondue pot. Adjust the flame so that the fondue bubbles lightly. Serve with the bread and/or vegetables.

*Makes 12 to 24 appetizer servings.*
*Makes 4 main course servings.*

# *B*UFFALO *C*HICKEN *W*INGS

In this version, the wings taste especially good because they are baked, not fried. According to the Love Chef, Buffalo Chicken Wings were first served at the Anchor Bar in Buffalo, New York, in 1964. For mild wings, use just a dash of cayenne pepper; for hot wings, use ⅛ teaspoon cayenne; for red-hot wings, use ¼ teaspoon.

| | |
|---|---|
| 18 to 24 | chicken wings |
| ½ | cup unsalted margarine, melted |
| 6 | tablespoons hot pepper sauce |
| | Cayenne pepper to taste |
| | Celery sticks |
| | Blue cheese dressing of your choice |

■ Preheat the oven to 425° F.

■ Place the wings on a rack in a baking pan and bake for 10 minutes. Remove the pan from the oven and reduce the heat to 400° F.

■ In a small bowl, stir together the margarine, hot pepper sauce, and cayenne pepper. Remove a small amount of the sauce and brush it onto the wings.

■ Bake the wings for 10 to 12 minutes longer, or until crispy and cooked through. Pour the remaining sauce over the wings. Serve the wings with celery sticks and blue cheese dressing on the side.

*Makes 4 to 6 appetizer servings.*

## WHAT'S THE BEST THING ABOUT COOKING AT HOME?

**KATHIE LEE:** Frank's barbecue! Frank barbecues all winter long, too. In a snow storm, he's out there.

# *N*AUTICAL *NUGGETS*

Jennifer Trainer and Elizabeth Wheeler, the coauthors of *The Yachting Cookbook*, both have had a lot of experience cooking on the high seas. They developed this recipe on a 40-foot boat during a 10-day sail, from Maine to the British Virgin Islands. They say their challenge at sea is to create recipes that use the freshest ingredients with a minimum of fuss. This one would be wonderful for parties—especially kids' birthdays.

Jennifer appeared as the book's representative on "Live." Because a completed recipe must be ready for Regis to taste at the end of a cooking segment, Jennifer found herself (in curlers) at 5:30 A.M. in the basement kitchen of the appropriately named St. Regis Hotel, cooking up a hero batch of Nautical Nuggets alongside chefs who were preparing breakfast for room-service patrons.

| | |
|---|---|
| 6 | *boneless, skinless chicken breast halves* |
| | *Salt and freshly ground pepper to taste* |
| 1 | *teaspoon dried oregano leaves* |
| 1/2 | *cup sour cream or plain yogurt* |
| 2 | *tablespoons freshly squeezed lemon juice* |
| 1 | *teaspoon Tabasco* |
| 1 | *garlic clove, finely chopped* |
| 2 | *cups finely crushed saltines or Ritz crackers (about 40 crackers)* |
| 1/2 | *cup sesame seeds* |
| 1/4 | *cup (1/2 stick) unsalted butter, melted* |

▪ Remove the tender fillet part of each breast and place it in a bowl. Then cut each chicken breast diagonally into 3 strips and add these to the bowl. Season with salt, pepper, and oregano, rubbing the seasoning into the chicken.

▪ Add the sour cream, lemon juice, Tabasco, and garlic to the chicken in the bowl and turn the pieces until they are thoroughly coated. Cover the chicken and marinate for at least 1 hour, or refrigerate overnight.

▪ Preheat the oven to 400° F. Lightly oil a baking sheet.

▪ Spread the cracker crumbs and sesame seeds in a shallow dish. One at a time, roll each piece of chicken in the cracker-crumb mixture until evenly coated. Arrange the pieces on the prepared baking sheet so that they are barely touching. Drizzle the melted butter evenly over the chicken.

▪ Bake the chicken for about 20 minutes, or until golden brown. Serve hot or at room temperature.

*Makes 4 to 6 servings.*

**Variation:** Substitute pieces of firm fish such as cod, monkfish, or halibut for the chicken.

*Regis finds a way to be "on camera" even during a break!*

# VEGETABLE EGG ROLLS

Cookbook author Jenifer Lang made a batch of these egg rolls on "Live" and served them to a discriminating tasting panel of six babies in high chairs, including her own son, Simon. While these egg rolls would be a fine adult appetizer, they are especially good for kids because they are individual little packages (which kids love!) and they are filled with nutritious things such as tofu and vegetables. (It's also a great way to get children to eat foods that they normally won't touch.) *Jenifer Lang Cooks for Kids* has all sorts of other recipes, too, that will appeal to youngsters. Egg-roll wrappers (and wonton wrappers) and tofu can be found in the produce section of your supermarket.

| | |
|---|---|
| 4 | tablespoons vegetable oil, divided |
| 1/4 | cup finely chopped scallions, including the tender green tops |
| 1 | teaspoon finely chopped fresh ginger root |
| 1 | cup diced carrots |
| 1/2 | cup bean sprouts or diced celery |
| 1/2 | cup frozen chopped spinach, thawed and drained |
| 1/4 | cup chicken broth |
| 2 | tablespoons reduced-sodium soy sauce |
| 1 | tablespoon granulated sugar |
| 4 | ounces soft or firm tofu |
| 10 | egg-roll wrappers, each cut in half diagonally, or 20 wonton wrappers |

▪ In a wok or large skillet, heat 2 tablespoons of the oil over low heat. Cook the scallions and ginger for about 10 minutes, or until the scallions are translucent and wilted, stirring occasionally.

▪ Add the carrots and bean sprouts or celery and stir-fry over high heat for 2 minutes. Add the spinach, broth, soy sauce, and sugar and bring the mixture to a boil. Reduce the heat and simmer for 10 to 15 minutes, or until the vegetables are soft, stirring occasionally. Cool for at least 15 minutes. Place the mixture in the container of a food processor fitted with a metal chopping blade, add the tofu, and process to the desired texture. (You can make the filling up to 2 days ahead and fill and fry the egg rolls as needed.)

▪ Place 1 tablespoon of the filling diagonally on each wrapper. Fold 1 corner over the filling. Then fold the 2 sides in to form an open envelope. Moisten the edge of the last flap with a little water and roll over until the flap is completely wound around the filling.

▪ In another skillet, heat the remaining 2 tablespoons of oil over medium-high heat and cook the egg rolls until they are golden brown on all sides, using tongs to turn them. Serve when cool enough to eat.

*Makes 20 appetizers.*

**Variations**: You can substitute any kind of fresh or frozen vegetables in this recipe if you make sure that the volume adds up to the same amount that is called for in the recipe. You can also use leftover Chinese food, either vegetables or a meat-and-vegetable combination. Grind it in the food processor with or without some tofu and follow the filling and cooking instructions.

Steve Friedman/Buena Vista Television

*Stage manager Julian Abio enjoys Kathie Lee's playful banter as she introduces Michael Gelman to the audience.*

# ROBIN LEACH'S
# MEDITERRANEAN EGGPLANT PIE

During Bachelor Cooking Week on "Live," Robin Leach created this delectable recipe, packed with vegetables—and topped with as much caviar as you can afford! Of course, he recommends accompanying it with champagne—both while you are making it and when you serve it—and both he and Regis were sipping from flutes of champagne as they put this layered delight together. For almost 200 "Robin Leach Recommended" recipes, don't miss his new *The Lifestyles of the Rich and Famous Cookbook.*

| | |
|---|---|
| 1 | *medium eggplant, cut into ¼-inch-thick slices* |
| | *Salt and freshly ground black pepper to taste* |
| 2 | *tablespoons olive oil* |
| 2 | *large onions, sliced* |
| 1 | *package (10 ounces) fresh spinach, cleaned and trimmed of stems* |
| 2 | *medium tomatoes, peeled and sliced* |
| ¾ | *cup homemade or store-bought pesto sauce* |
| | *Unbaked pastry crust for a single (10-inch) pie* |
| | *Black or golden caviar, for serving with the baked pie* |

▪ Preheat the oven to 400° F. Lightly butter a 2¾-quart deep baking dish (such as a soufflé dish) that is 8 to 9 inches in diameter.

▪ Season the eggplant with salt and pepper. Set aside.

▪ In a large skillet, heat the oil over medium heat. Add the onions and cook for 10 to 15 minutes, or until the onions are softened but not browned. Set aside.

▪ Place the washed spinach in a large saucepot. Cover, and cook over high heat for 3 to 5 minutes, or until the spinach is wilted. Squeeze as much moisture as you can out of the spinach.

▪ Arrange half of the eggplant in the bottom of the prepared dish. Top with layers of half the onions, spinach, tomatoes, and pesto sauce. Repeat the layers with the remaining ingredients, ending with the pesto sauce.

▪ Roll out the pastry on a lightly floured surface until it is about ¼ inch thick and large enough to cover the top of the casserole. Place it on top of the casserole. If you like, you can form a raised edge around the pastry or decorate the top.

▪ Bake for 50 to 60 minutes, or until golden brown and heated through. Let stand for 15 minutes. Serve the vegetables with a piece of the crust and top each serving with caviar.

*Makes 8 servings.*

# SESAME BAY SCALLOPS

The Love Chef returned to the show in April of 1991 with this dish he dedicated to "spring fever." Serve this either as a hot or cold appetizer or as a main course over rice or pasta.

    2    *tablespoons Oriental-style sesame oil*
  1½    *pounds bay scallops (or sea scallops cut into quarters)*
    ½    *pound fresh snow peas*
    2    *jars (4.5 ounces each) button mushrooms*
    1    *carrot, peeled and cut into julienne strips*
    2    *tablespoons sesame seeds*
    1    *teaspoon ground coriander*
         *Lemon slices and watercress sprigs, for garnish (optional)*

▪ Heat a large skillet or wok over medium-high heat. Add the oil. Cook the scallops for 3 minutes, stirring frequently. Add the snow peas, mushrooms, and carrots and cook for 3 to 4 minutes longer, or until the carrots are just crisp-tender, stirring frequently. Remove the skillet or wok from the heat. Add the sesame seeds and coriander and toss to combine.

▪ Cover and refrigerate until chilled or serve hot over pasta or rice. Garnish with lemon slices and watercress sprigs, if desired.

*Makes 8 appetizer servings or 4 main dish servings.*

# Chef Tell's Fast and Fabulous Hors D'oeuvres

Chef Tell Erhardt frequently appears on "Live with Regis & Kathie Lee." Although his birth name is Friedman Paul Erhardt, he gained the nickname "Tell" because he appeared in school plays as the Swiss hero, William Tell. He began his culinary career at the age of 14 and received his first major award at the age of 27, when he won a gold medal at the Culinary Olympics and was named Chef of the Year.

These recipes use ingredients that are often on hand or are left over from meals.

### Ham Rolls

▪ Place a slice of ham on a plate and spread mustard over the ham. You can also flavor mayonnaise with a little curry powder and use it in place of the mustard. Place a cooked spear of asparagus on the ham and roll the ham around the asparagus.

### Ham Cornets

▪ In the container of a food processor fitted with the metal chopping blade, process 2 cups of cream cheese, ½ cup of prepared horseradish, and a dash of lemon juice until blended. Place the mixture in a pastry bag that is fitted with a star tip. Roll slices of ham into cone shapes and pipe the mixture into the ham.

### Spicy Ham Spread

▪ In the container of a food processor fitted with the metal chopping blade, process 2 cups of chopped ham, 1 tablespoon of prepared horse-radish, and ½ cup of mayonnaise until blended. Using a rolling pin, lightly roll over slices of fresh bread to flatten them slightly. Spread the ham mixture on the bread. Roll the bread up and then cut each piece in half.

### LEFTOVER CHEESE BALLS

- In the container of a food processor fitted with the metal chopping blade, process leftover cheese pieces (any type), adding softened butter, if necessary, to create a mixture that holds together. Form the mixture into small balls and roll each ball in chopped nuts or bread crumbs. Refrigerate until ready to serve.

### LEFTOVER CHEESE SPREAD

- In the container of a food processor fitted with the metal chopping blade, process 1 cup of hard cheese pieces, ½ cup of soft cheese, ½ cup (1 stick) of butter, and 2 tablespoons of brandy until blended. Place the mixture in a pastry bag that is fitted with a star tip. Pipe the mixture onto celery, split dates, crackers, or slices of miniature bread.

### STUFFED EGGS

- In the container of a food processor fitted with the metal chopping blade, process together 2 ounces of cream cheese for every 4 hard-cooked egg yolks until blended. Spoon the mixture into the egg-white halves and sprinkle the tops with paprika.

## HOW TO MAKE PERFECT HARD-COOKED EGGS

Place the eggs in a saucepan that comfortably holds the number you are cooking. Fill the pan with just enough cold water so that the water comes about 1 inch over the tops of the eggs. Bring the pan of water to a boil. Turn off the heat and cover the pan. Let stand for 15 minutes.

Drain the eggs and immediately place them in a bowl of cold water. When the eggs have cooled, gently crack them on a hard, flat surface to loosen the shells. Starting at the large end where there is an air space, peel off the shell and the thin white membrane. Dip the egg in cold water occasionally to help.

TIP: If you don't know if an egg is hard-cooked or raw, simply spin it on a flat surface. If it wobbles, it's cooked; if it spins evenly, it's raw.

## *Stuffed Eggs Variations:*

▪ Add 1 roasted red bell pepper to the processor with the cream cheese and yolks and process until smooth. Garnish each egg with a sliver of red pepper.

▪ Add 2 to 3 shrimp and a dash of lemon juice to the processor with the cream cheese and yolks and process until smooth. Garnish each egg with a shrimp.

▪ Add ½ ripe avocado and a dash of lemon juice to the processor with the cream cheese and yolks and process until smooth. Garnish each egg with a sliver of avocado.

▪ Chop 1 small onion and cook it in a skillet with a little butter until it is softened. Add the cooked onion to the processor with the cream cheese and yolks and process until smooth. Garnish with additional cooked onion.

# Soup's On

# CLEVER LETTUCE SOUP

The Clever Cleaver Brothers (two macho-looking chefs) always dress in unique costumes and introduce their segments with rap lyrics. They really aren't brothers, but they sure are clever! This flavorful and low-calorie soup recipe is one of their many inspired creations.

| | |
|---|---|
| ½ | *head iceberg lettuce, cut into 1-inch pieces (about 4 cups)* |
| ½ | *head romaine lettuce, cut into 1-inch pieces (about 4 cups)* |
| 1 | *medium Spanish onion, chopped* |
| 3 | *cups chicken broth, divided* |
| 1 | *teaspoon curry powder* |
| ¼ to ½ | *teaspoon coarsely ground black pepper* |
| ⅛ | *teaspoon low-sodium Worcestershire sauce* |

▪ In a large saucepan, combine the lettuces, onion, and 2¾ cups of the chicken broth. In a small bowl, stir together the remaining ¼ cup of broth, curry powder, pepper, and Worcestershire sauce. Stir the curry powder mixture into the lettuce mixture.

▪ Heat the soup over medium-high heat until it comes to a boil. Reduce the heat to low and simmer for 15 minutes.

▪ In a blender or a food processor fitted with the metal chopping blade, process the soup until it is almost smooth, but still has some texture. (If you use a blender, process the soup in small batches.) Reheat, if necessary, and serve immediately.

*Makes 4 servings.*

# Sensational Chicken Soup

Once the chef for New York City's gourmet mayor, Ed Koch, Rozanne Gold is now the culinary director of the Joseph Baum and Michael Whiteman Company, a restaurant group that manages the acclaimed Rainbow Room atop the Big Apple's Rockefeller Center. "Live" gave Rozanne the challenge of preparing a dish that would be equally appropriate for Passover or Easter. Her solution was this versatile soup recipe. Regis's contribution to the segment was creating a matzoh softball.

### BASIC SOUP

| | |
|---|---|
| 6 | cans (13¾ ounces each) chicken broth |
| 1 | pound chicken backs, wings, and necks |
| 3 | carrots, chopped |
| 2 | leeks, chopped |
| 2 | celery ribs, chopped |
| 1 | turnip or parsnip, chopped |
| 1 | red onion, chopped |
| ¼ | cup chopped parsley |
| 2 | garlic cloves, finely chopped |
| 2 | teaspoons dried basil leaves |

### PASSOVER ADDITION

| | |
|---|---|
| 12 to 16 | matzoh balls |

### EASTER ADDITIONS

| | |
|---|---|
| 2 | cups freshly cooked orzo |
| | Juice of 1 lemon |
| ¼ | cup chopped fresh dill |

▪ Pour all of the chicken broth into a large saucepot. Bring the broth to a boil over high heat. Add the remaining ingredients, cover, reduce the heat to low, and cook for 1 hour.

▪ Remove all the chicken bones. Cook the soup over high heat for 10 minutes longer.

▪ Add the "addition" of your choice and serve.

*Makes 6 to 8 servings.*

# DOWN-HOME SPLIT PEA SOUP

The Love Chef, Francis Anthony, made this soul-satisfying soup on a cold January day. This is a wonderfully aromatic recipe to make on a wintry weekend.

|  |  |
|---|---|
| 1 | pound dry split green peas |
| 1½ | quarts chicken broth |
| 2 | large smoked ham hocks |
| 2 | cups milk |
| 1 | large onion, chopped |
| 1 | large potato, peeled and diced |
| 2 | bay leaves |
| 1 to 2 | tablespoons fresh dill |
| 3 | dashes of hot pepper sauce |
|  | Freshly ground black pepper to taste |

▪ Rinse the split peas and combine them with all the remaining ingredients in a large pot. Bring the mixture to a boil over high heat. Reduce the heat and bring the liquid just to a simmer. Cover and cook for 1 hour, stirring occasionally.

▪ Remove the cover and cook for an additional ½ hour. Remove the ham hocks. Slice the meat off the bones and cut it into bite-size pieces. Discard the fat, bones and bay leaves. Return the meat to the pot and cook ½ hour longer.

*Makes about 2 quarts.*

# BOWL OF THE WIFE OF KIT CARSON

Sam'l P. Arnold, cookbook author and owner of The Fort, a restaurant near Denver that specializes in Western American cuisine, prepared a very special soup from his restaurant on "Live." He first became acquainted with this recipe in the 1960s when the late Leona Wood, granddaughter of Kit Carson, worked at The Fort and reported that this soup was a favorite with Josefa Carson, her grandmother. While Sam's arrival in the Big Apple went without a hitch, his trip back to Colorado was pretty wild—the power went out in the New York City airports, and he had to sit in a sweltering plane for seven hours. Released at midnight, he then had to find a hotel room for the remainder of the night. A day later, Sam finally got a plane back to Denver—where we hope he enjoyed a bowl of this delicious soup accompanied by red wine and a good crusty bread.

4   cups chicken broth
1   cup shredded cooked chicken or turkey
1   cup cooked rice
1   cup cooked or canned garbanzos
1   chipotle pepper, seeded and finely chopped
    Pinch of dried oregano leaves
1   avocado, peeled and cut into slices
1   cup diced Monterey jack cheese

▪ In a 2-quart saucepan, bring the broth to a boil over high heat. Add the chicken, rice, garbanzos, chipotle pepper, and oregano and cook for about 5 minutes longer, or until heated through.

▪ Serve in individual bowls and top each serving with avocado and cheese.

*Makes 6 servings.*

# NEW ENGLAND CLAM CHOWDER

Legal Sea Foods sells about 1,500 gallons a week of their flavorful chowder at their eight restaurants and take-out counters. Now, with the help of co-owner Roger Berkowitz, you can create their special blend at home. Roger says that the reason the chowder is so popular is because they "use only the best ingredients and plenty of them." He advises that you shouldn't try to economize and cut back on the amount of clams or cream. During Roger's demonstration on "Live," he was going to add lard to the recipe. Kathie Lee, who was pregnant at the time, said, "I'll show you lard!" and gave everyone a "hip check."

4   *quarts littleneck clams*
1   *cup water*
1   *garlic clove, finely chopped*
2   *ounces salt pork, finely chopped*
2   *cups chopped onions*
3   *tablespoons all-purpose flour*
4½   *cups clam broth*
3   *cups fish stock*
1½   *pounds potatoes, peeled and diced*
2   *cups light cream*
  *Oyster crackers, for serving with the chowder (optional)*

▪ Scrub the clams well to remove any surface grit. In a large covered saucepot over medium-high heat, heat the water to boiling. Add the clams and garlic and cook for 6 to 10 minutes, or until the clams have just opened. Drain the clams, reserving the broth. Strain the broth through coffee filters or several layers of cheesecloth to remove any traces of grit. Remove the clams from their shells and chop them finely.

*Steve Friedman/Buena Vista Television*

*Is there a doctor in the house?*

■ In a large heavy saucepot, cook the salt pork over low heat until the fat is rendered and becomes liquid. Using a slotted spoon, remove the "cracklings" and reserve them.

■ Add the onions to the fat and cook over medium-high heat for 5 to 7 minutes, or until softened but not browned. Stir in the flour and cook for 3 minutes, stirring constantly. Add the reserved clam broth, the 4½ cups of clam broth, and the fish stock, whisking to remove any lumps. Bring the liquid to a boil, then add the potatoes, reduce the heat, and simmer for about 15 minutes, or until the potatoes are cooked through.

■ Stir in the reserved clams, salt pork cracklings, and the light cream. Heat the chowder until it is the temperature you prefer. Serve the chowder in large soup bowls with oyster crackers, if desired.

*Makes 8 servings.*

# SUPER BOWL CHILI

Phillip Stephen Schulz appeared on "Live" just before the 1990 Super Bowl to promote his cookbook, *As American as Apple Pie*. Phillip's book has an entire chapter on chili and, though he himself is a Denver Broncos fan, he made this particular version, which came from Jill Gardner in San Francisco (appropriately, because San Francisco turned out to be the winning team). Just reading the list of ingredients for this chili should make you head for the kitchen. Goat cheese and parsley add to the flavor of Phillip's savory mixture.

| | |
|---|---|
| 3 | dried ancho chilies (or dried poblanos) |
| 1 | tablespoon vegetable oil |
| 2½ | pounds beef chuck, cut into ½-inch cubes |
| 1 | large onion, chopped |
| 2 | garlic cloves, chopped |
| 1½ | cups beef broth |
| ½ | cup dry white wine |
| 1 | tablespoon tomato paste |
| 1 | teaspoon ground cumin |
| ½ | teaspoon dried oregano leaves, crushed |
| | Salt and pepper to taste |
| | Crumbled goat cheese, for garnish |
| | Chopped fresh parsley, for garnish |

■ Remove the stems and seeds from the chilies. Place them in a small saucepan and add enough water just to cover them. Bring the mixture to a boil, then reduce the heat to low and simmer for 15 minutes. Set aside to cool for about 5 minutes.

■ In the container of a blender or a food processor fitted with a metal chopping blade, process the chilies and ½ cup of the liquid until smooth.

Steve Friedman/Buena Vista Television

*Regis and Kathie Lee share a quiet moment while Michael Gelman and Director of Programming Art Moore discuss details for the upcoming show.*

▪ In a large saucepot, heat the oil over medium-high heat. Add the beef and cook for about 10 to 15 minutes, or until the beef is browned, stirring frequently. Transfer the beef to a plate and reserve.

▪ Add the onion and garlic and cook for 4 to 5 minutes until softened, stirring frequently. Return the reserved beef to the pot.

▪ Stir in the chilies, beef broth, white wine, tomato paste, cumin, and oregano. Heat to a boil. Reduce the heat to low, cover, and simmer for about 1½ hours, or until the beef is tender, stirring occasionally. Season with salt and pepper. Garnish with goat cheese and parsley.

*Makes 4 to 6 servings.*

# PHYLLIS DILLER'S OYSTER STEW

Comedienne Phyllis Diller has known Regis for over 35 years and is one of his and Kathie Lee's biggest fans. When she appeared on "Live" in December 1988, she was all set to make this scrumptious soup recipe she got from her mother. When she arrived on the day of the show, she remembers, the crew "had not found any *cans* of oysters. They sent out a whole bunch of guys in all directions and they finally found—*small* cans of *small* oysters. Evidently they aren't just everywhere on the shelves in New York City." If *you* have trouble finding cans of oysters, with a little extra effort you can substitute fresh oysters in Phyllis's soup-like stew. Add a little clam broth or fish stock to make up the oyster juice.

3    *cups canned oysters*
½    *cup (1 stick) butter*
1½   *quarts low-fat milk*
1    *teaspoon salt*
1    *teaspoon cracked black pepper*
     *Soda crackers to serve with the soup*

▪ Drain the oysters and reserve the juice to add to the soup.

▪ In a large saucepot, heat the butter over medium-high heat. Add the drained oysters and cook for 3 to 5 minutes, or until heated through.

▪ Add the reserved juice, milk, salt, and pepper. Stir occasionally and continue to cook just until hot. (Do not allow the stew to boil or the oysters will be rubbery.) Serve with soda crackers.

*Makes 10 to 12 servings.*

# VEGETABLE SOUP

———■□■———

Jane Brody is health and nutrition columnist for *The New York Times*, and while on "Live" she made this recipe from her cookbook, *Good Food Gourmet*. It seems the recipe was sent to Jane by one of her readers, Marcia Flammonde of Stroudsburg, Pennsylvania, who created this simple soup for the annual Autumnal Peasant Dinner, which the folks there give to salute Pocono mountain poetry (the fall colors) and Professor Richard Leland, "who inspires culinary creativity."

|          |                                                              |
|----------|--------------------------------------------------------------|
| 3        | cups chicken broth (preferably homemade or unsalted)          |
| 2        | Granny Smith apples, peeled and cut into ¾-inch cubes         |
| 2        | carrots, peeled and sliced                                    |
| 2        | parsnips, peeled and sliced                                   |
| 6        | ounces rutabaga, peeled and cut into ¾-inch cubes            |
| 1        | onion, peeled and sliced                                      |
| ½        | cup chopped fennel bulb                                       |
| ⅓        | cup chopped green beans (fresh or frozen)                     |
| ½        | teaspoon ground cinnamon                                      |
| ¼        | teaspoon ground cloves                                        |
| ¼        | teaspoon freshly grated nutmeg                                |
| 2 to 3   | cups water, as needed (optional)                              |
|          | Salt to taste (optional)                                      |
|          | Freshly ground black pepper to taste                         |
|          | Fennel leaves, for garnish (optional)                        |

▪ In a large saucepot, combine the broth, apples, carrots, parsnips, rutabaga, onion, fennel, green beans, cinnamon, cloves, and nutmeg. Bring the ingredients to a boil over medium heat. Cover the pot, reduce the heat, and simmer for 35 to 45 minutes, or until the vegetables are tender.

▪ Puree the soup in several batches in a blender or a food processor fitted with a metal chopping blade. (Make sure to hold the lid on tightly if you are using a blender.) Return the puree to the saucepot and stir in enough of the water to achieve the desired consistency. Season the soup with salt and pepper and heat it thoroughly. Garnish with fennel leaves, if desired.

*Makes 6 to 8 servings.*

# HEARTY RED LENTIL LEMON SOUP

▬▬

Annemarie Colbin was early in finishing the preparations for her demonstration and left the pot of soup on the stage's hot stove top for more than an hour. When it was finally time for her segment, the soup had thickened to the consistency of porridge. Regis's comment was, "That's thick!" Annemarie had no water to thin it with, so she replied, "It's supposed to be hearty." Annemarie is director of the Natural Gourmet Institute for Food and Health and author of *The Natural Gourmet*, in which the original version of this substantial soup appears. Annemarie created the recipe with the help of 12 of her students at the institute.

|     |                                                      |
| --- | ---------------------------------------------------- |
| 2   | tablespoons olive oil                                |
| 1   | large Spanish onion, finely chopped                  |
| 3   | garlic cloves, finely chopped                        |
| 1½  | teaspoons ground cumin                               |
| 5   | cups water                                           |
| 1½  | cups red lentils                                     |
| 2   | 2-inch-by-½-inch strips of lemon peel                |
| 1   | teaspoon sea salt or to taste                        |
| 1   | bay leaf                                             |
| 1   | tablespoon freshly squeezed lemon juice              |
| 6   | lemon slices, for garnish                            |

▪ In a 4-quart saucepan, heat the oil over medium-high heat. Cook the onion for 2 to 3 minutes, stirring frequently. Add the garlic and cumin and cook for 5 to 7 minutes longer, or until golden.

▪ Add the water to the pan. Rinse the lentils quickly and add the lentils, lemon peels, salt, and bay leaf. Reduce the heat, cover the pan, and simmer for 25 minutes, or until the lentils are tender. Discard the bay leaf and lemon peels. Stir in the lemon juice.

▪ Serve in heated soup bowls and garnish each serving with a slice of lemon.

*Makes 6 servings.*

# *Pasta Possibilities*

# PAPARDELLE WITH SAUSAGE

Stephen Goebel is director of food and beverage for Sfuzzi, Inc., a chain of 14 restaurants. The first Sfuzzi restaurant opened in Dallas and was such a success that Sfuzzi now seems to be taking over the country. Papardelle is a broad noodle (lasagna can also be used).

1   tablespoon olive oil
1   teaspoon finely chopped garlic
2   pounds Italian sausage, chopped and cooked
2   cups peeled, seeded, and diced plum tomatoes
1   cup oil-packed sun-dried tomatoes, drained
2   cups marinara sauce
1   pound papardelle or lasagna pasta, cooked according to package
      directions and drained
2   tablespoons butter
    Salt and pepper to taste
    Grated Parmesan cheese to taste
    Chopped parsley to taste

▪ In a large saucepot, heat the oil over medium-high heat. Cook the garlic for 1 to 3 minutes, or until the garlic is translucent, stirring constantly.

▪ Add the sausage and both kinds of tomatoes and cook, stirring frequently, until the mixture is heated through. Add the marinara sauce and bring the mixture to a boil. Remove the pot from the heat.

▪ Add the pasta to the sauce and heat through. Stir in the butter, salt, pepper, Parmesan, and parsley.

*Makes 8 servings.*

# LINGUINE WITH SWEET RED PEPPER SAUCE

Laurie Burrows Grad's first experience of cooking on television was on "A.M. Los Angeles," when Regis was the host. On this segment for "Live," Laurie told Regis to test the pasta for doneness by throwing it against the wall. If it sticks to the wall, it is too gummy and therefore not done. As you might guess, Regis and Laurie spent most of the segment throwing linguine at the walls!

Try this recipe next time you are looking for a recipe that is low in fat, low in calories, and high in fiber. The flavorful red pepper sauce is prepared with only one tablespoon of olive oil. The secret ingredient is a thinly sliced pear cooked in the sauce, which adds just a touch of natural sweetness. Laurie recommends serving this dish with a salad of watercress with orange segments and red onion, and a whole-wheat popover.

|       |                                                                                  |
|-------|----------------------------------------------------------------------------------|
| 1     | tablespoon olive oil                                                             |
| 4     | red bell peppers, seeded and cut into julienne strips                            |
| 2     | carrots, finely chopped                                                          |
| 2     | cups crushed tomatoes packed in puree                                            |
| ½     | ripe Anjou, Bartlett, or Comice pear, peeled and thinly sliced                   |
| 1     | tablespoon freshly chopped basil or ½ teaspoon dried crushed basil leaves        |
| 1     | teaspoon finely chopped garlic                                                   |
|       | Salt and freshly ground pepper to taste                                          |
| 1     | pound dried linguine, cooked according to package directions and drained         |
| 2     | tablespoons grated Parmesan cheese, for garnish                                  |
| 2     | tablespoons chopped parsley, for garnish                                         |

▪ In a large non-stick saucepan, heat the oil over medium heat. Add the peppers and carrots and cook for 7 to 10 minutes, or until the vegetables are softened slightly.

## HOW TO COOK PERFECT PASTA

**1.** Use plenty of water when you are cooking pasta—at least 1 quart for every 4 ounces of dry pasta. Bring the water to a fast boil in an uncovered pot. A rapid boil helps circulate the pasta for even cooking. Add a little salt, unless you must avoid it for health reasons.

**2.** While the pasta is cooking, use a wooden fork or a similar utensil and stir frequently to separate the strands or pieces.

**3.** Follow the package directions! Cook pasta to the degree of tenderness desired, from tender to fairly firm (al dente).

**4.** Drain the pasta in a colander to stop the cooking action. Do not rinse the pasta unless the recipe specifically says to do so. Stir in 1 to 2 tablespoons of butter or olive oil to prevent the cooked pasta from sticking together.

▪ Add the tomatoes, pear, basil, garlic, salt, and pepper. Bring the mixture to a boil, cover, reduce the heat, and simmer for 45 minutes, or until very tender.

▪ Adjust the seasonings in the sauce. (If you like, you can puree the sauce before tossing it with the pasta.) Toss the pasta with the sauce and serve it hot, garnished with Parmesan cheese and parsley.

*Makes 6 servings.*

*Variations*: If tomatoes packed in puree are unavailable, use regular whole juice-packed tomatoes. Chop the tomatoes and drain off most of the liquid. Return the tomatoes to the can and fill it to the top with canned tomato puree.

If you like, you can substitute 2 yellow bell peppers for 2 of the red bell peppers.

# PASTA WITH CRAWFISH, SHRIMP, OR CRABMEAT IN CREAM SAUCE

Frequent guest Chef Paul Prudhomme was on "Live" most recently to promote his third cookbook, *Chef Paul Prudhomme's Seasoned America*. In addition to being a cookbook author, Chef Paul runs a very successful restaurant in New Orleans called K-Paul's Louisiana Kitchen and produces his own line of seasonings called Magic Seasoning Blends™.

This is an easy, yet elegant recipe that is perfect for entertaining. If you want to add even more flavor to this dish, include ¼ cup diced smoked ham, preferably Tasso (a highly seasoned Cajun smoked ham) or Cure 81.

| | |
|---|---|
| ⅓ | *pound uncooked thin spaghetti or rotelli* |
| 6 | *tablespoons unsalted butter or margarine* |
| 1 | *tablespoon Chef Paul Prudhomme's Seafood Magic®* |
| ¼ | *cup finely chopped scallions* |
| 2 | *cups heavy cream or half-and-half* |
| 1 | *pound crawfish tails; or peeled, raw medium shrimp; or crabmeat* |

■ Cook the spaghetti according to the package directions just to the al dente stage. Immediately drain the pasta and rinse with hot water to wash off the starch, then with cold water to stop the cooking process. Drain again. (To prevent the pasta from sticking together, pour a very small amount of oil into the palm of your hand and rub it through the pasta after rinsing.)

■ In a large skillet, melt the butter over medium heat. Add the Seafood Magic® and scallions and sauté for 1 to 2 minutes, stirring occasionally. Gradually add the cream or half-and-half while either stirring or shaking the pan in a back-and-forth motion until the mixture comes to a boil. Simmer over medium heat, continuing to shake the pan, until the sauce thickens somewhat, about 2 to 3 minutes.

▪ Add the seafood and bring to a boil. Add the freshly cooked spaghetti; toss and stir for about 2 minutes, or until the spaghetti is heated through. Do not overcook the seafood. Serve immediately.

*Makes 2 main-dish or 4 side-dish servings.*

# Bat-Wing Pasta

Joyce Steins, who is the owner of Le Bar Bat and Café Iguana in New York City, appeared on "Live" at Halloween with her solution to "treat overdose"—give the kids a hearty and healthy dinner they love that will fill them up enough to delay a candy binge. As honorary Bat Lady of the day, Joyce said the peanut butter and the bowtie-shaped pasta in this recipe are the key ingredients that give you the edge in tempting your little ghosts and goblins.

| | |
|---|---|
| 3 | *tablespoons plus 1 teaspoon vegetable oil* |
| 3/4 | *pound uncooked chicken, diced* |
| | *Salt and pepper to taste* |
| 1 | *garlic clove, finely chopped* |
| 3/4 | *cup chicken broth* |
| 1 | *teaspoon granulated sugar* |
| 1 | *cup peanut butter* |
| 1/4 | *cup sesame paste* |
| 2 | *teaspoons soy sauce* |
| 1 | *pound bowtie pasta, cooked according to package directions and drained* |
| 1/2 | *cucumber, peeled and chopped* |
| 1/2 | *cup plain peanuts, chopped* |
| 2 | *scallions, finely chopped* |

▪ In a large saucepan, heat 3 tablespoons of the oil over medium-high heat. Cook the chicken for 3 to 5 minutes, or until no longer pink, stirring frequently. Season with salt and pepper.

▪ In another saucepan, heat the remaining teaspoon of oil over medium-high heat. Cook the garlic for about 1 minute, or until lightly golden, stirring constantly. Add the chicken broth and the sugar and bring to a boil. Gradually add the peanut butter, stirring constantly until the mixture is smooth and creamy. Stir in the sesame paste and soy sauce until smooth.

▪ Add the peanut butter sauce to the chicken and simmer for about 5 minutes. Mix in the pasta "bat wings" and toss to coat. Sprinkle the top with cucumber, peanuts, and scallions.

*Makes 4 to 6 servings.*

# Santa Fe Chili Pasta

Tommy Tang, cookbook author, bicoastal restaurant-owner, and chef, appeared on "Live" to prepare the recipe that follows, which is equally appreciated in both the Los Angeles and New York Tommy Tang's. Tommy says his customers "order it by the tons!" Look in Asian specialty markets for several of the ingredients called for in this recipe. Tommy likes to serve pasta as a second course between the appetizer and the entree.

> 3   *tablespoons olive oil*
> 2   *tablespoons finely chopped red onion*
> 1   *tablespoon finely chopped garlic*
> 1   *tablespoon chili powder*
> 2   *teaspoons roasted chili paste*
> 1   *cup coconut milk*
> 1½  *teaspoons Thai fish sauce or ¼ teaspoon salt*
> 1   *cup heavy cream*
> 12  *ounces penne pasta, cooked according to package directions and drained*
> 4   *sun-dried tomatoes, packed in oil, drained and cut into ¼-inch strips*
> 4   *sprigs fresh basil or cilantro, for garnish*

Steve Friedman/Buena Vista Television

*Tommy Tang and Regis swap stories between recipes.*

▪ In a large skillet, heat the oil over medium-high heat. Cook the onion and garlic for 5 to 7 minutes, or until lightly browned.

▪ Add the chili powder and roasted chili paste and cook and stir for 1 minute. Add the coconut milk and fish sauce and bring to a boil. Stir in the cream and return the mixture to a boil. Reduce the heat to low and simmer for 5 minutes, stirring every minute. Increase the heat to medium. Add the pasta and stir until the pasta is well coated with the sauce. Transfer the mixture to a warm platter and top with the sun-dried tomatoes. Garnish with basil or cilantro, and serve.

*Makes 4 servings.*

# PARTY PASTA SALAD

No summer party would be complete without this pasta salad from Chef Tell. You can serve it with or without the chicken; it's also good with seafood.

### PASTA SALAD

$^{1}/_{2}$ cup red wine vinegar
$^{1}/_{2}$ cup olive oil
2 tablespoons finely chopped fresh basil leaves
Finely chopped garlic to taste
Salt and pepper to taste
1 pound pasta, cooked according to package directions and drained
1 tomato, peeled, seeded, and diced
$^{1}/_{2}$ cup grated Parmesan cheese
$^{1}/_{4}$ cup pitted black olives
Lettuce leaves

### MARINATED CHICKEN BREAST

$^{1}/_{4}$ cup teriyaki sauce
Dash of freshly grated ginger root or ground ginger to taste
1 (8-ounce) boneless, skinless chicken breast
1 tablespoon vegetable oil
Sprigs of parsley or basil, for garnish

▪ *To make the pasta salad:* In a large bowl, stir together the vinegar, oil, basil, garlic, salt, and pepper. Add the pasta, tomato, Parmesan cheese, and olives and toss to thoroughly combine. Let the salad stand for 1 hour. Serve on top of lettuce leaves.

▪ *To make the chicken breast:* In a medium bowl, stir together the teriyaki sauce and ginger. Add the chicken, cover, and refrigerate for 1 hour.

▪ In a large skillet, heat the oil over medium-high heat. Cook the chicken for 5 to 7 minutes on each side, or until cooked through.

▪ Slice the chicken into ½-inch-wide strips and place them on top of the pasta. Garnish with sprigs of parsley or basil.

*Makes 6 to 8 servings.*

# LINDA DANO'S MARINARA SAUCE

Popular daytime television personality Linda Dano has played Felicia Gallant on NBC's "Another World" for 10 years. Linda was also the original host of "Attitudes," a show she hosted for more than six years. She loves to cook and this recipe, like Linda, is authentically Italian. Linda says that she often uses it when cooking for her husband because it is quick and delicious. You can use it to enjoy the bounty of a home garden or adapt it to the canned tomatoes and dried basil leaves you have on your kitchen shelves.

1    *tablespoon olive oil*
2    *garlic cloves, finely chopped*
8    *ripe plum tomatoes, chopped*
10   *fresh basil leaves, torn*
1    *teaspoon granulated sugar*
     *Salt to taste*
1    *pound pasta, cooked according to package directions and drained*
     *Ricotta cheese, additional chopped tomatoes, and fresh basil*
       *leaves, for garnish*

▪ In a large saucepan, heat the oil over medium-high heat. Cook the garlic for 1 to 3 minutes, or until browned. Add the tomatoes, basil, sugar, and salt. Reduce the heat to medium and simmer for 10 to 15 minutes, stirring frequently.

▪ Serve the sauce over freshly cooked pasta. Top with ricotta cheese, chopped tomatoes, and basil leaves, for garnish.

*Makes 4 servings.*

# PASTA CON AMORE

Culinary pro Francis Anthony, the Love Chef, has his recipes available in a multitude of ways—in his book *Cooking with Love*, on videotape, and as a computerized recipe system (see the Resources section in the back of the book). This flavorful pasta dish is just one of his inspired creations.

| | |
|---|---|
| 6 | *tablespoons Italian olive oil* |
| 2 | *bunches scallions, chopped* |
| 1 | *small red bell pepper, seeded and chopped* |
| 1 | *very large ripe tomato, chopped* |
| 2 | *tablespoons capers* |
| 2 | *tablespoons chopped fresh basil or 1 tablespoon dried basil leaves* |
| 1 | *cup ricotta cheese* |
| | *Freshly ground black pepper and salt to taste* |
| 12 | *ounces ziti or penne pasta, cooked according to package directions and drained* |
| 4 | *ounces shredded mozzarella cheese* |

▪ In a large skillet, heat the olive oil over medium-high heat. Cook the scallions, red pepper, and tomato for 5 to 7 minutes, or until the vegetables are tender. Add the capers and basil and continue stirring. Add the ricotta, pepper, and salt. (If you like a smoother sauce, put the ricotta through a fine strainer/sieve before adding it to the pan.) Simmer until the ingredients are thoroughly blended.

▪ Divide the pasta among 4 plates and top with the sauce and the mozzarella. Serve immediately.

*Makes 4 servings.*

# FARFALLE À LA MARCELLO

When it comes to preparing Italian food, Marcello Sili is among the tops! He has been in the restaurant business for 42 years and currently is the owner of Marcello's in Harrington Park, New Jersey. For his appearance on "Live," Marcello selected this recipe because it is a good source of complex carbohydrates.

| | |
|---|---|
| 3 | tablespoons olive oil |
| 3 | garlic cloves, finely chopped |
| 1 | pound of assorted vegetables, cut into bite-size pieces |
| 20 | medium shrimp, peeled |
| | Pinch of salt and pepper |
| ¾ | cup chicken broth |
| | Splash of white wine |
| 2 | tablespoons mascarpone or cream cheese, softened |
| | Pinch of dried oregano leaves |
| 1 | pound bow-tie pasta, cooked according to package directions and drained |
| | Grated Parmesan cheese (optional) |

▪ In a large skillet, heat the oil over medium-high heat. Cook the garlic until lightly browned.

▪ Add the vegetables, shrimp, salt, and pepper and cook, stirring frequently, until the vegetables are crisp-tender and the shrimp is cooked through. Add the broth, white wine, mascarpone, and oregano and toss to combine. Toss the freshly cooked pasta with the vegetable mixture. Serve with grated Parmesan cheese, if desired.

*Makes 4 servings.*

# PASTA WITH BROCCOLI AND MUSHROOMS

Francis Anthony, the Love Chef, frequently appears on "Live With Regis & Kathie Lee." For more of his easy, pleasing recipes, make sure to check out his book, *Cooking with Love*.

| | |
|---|---|
| ½ | bunch broccoli |
| ¼ | cup olive oil |
| 7 | ounces mushrooms, sliced |
| 1 | medium red bell pepper, seeded and sliced into thin strips |
| 1 | garlic clove, peeled |
| ¼ | cup water |
| ¼ | cup dry white wine |
| 8 | ounces pasta, such as fettuccine or linguine |
| 2 | tablespoons unsalted butter |
| ½ | cup grated Parmesan cheese |
| | Freshly ground black pepper to taste |
| | Salt, if desired |

▪ Wash the broccoli. Trim off the leaves and tough ends of each stalk and peel the skin with a vegetable peeler. Cut the stalk into ½-inch pieces and the head into small florets.

▪ In a large skillet, heat the olive oil over medium heat. Add the broccoli, mushrooms, red pepper strips, and garlic; cook for 1 minute, stirring frequently. Discard the garlic when it is browned. Add the water and wine. Cover and cook over low heat for about 5 minutes, or until the broccoli is just tender but firm.

▪ Meanwhile, bring a large pot of salted water to a boil. Add the pasta and cook just until al dente. Drain the pasta thoroughly, return it to the saucepan, and toss with the butter. Stir in the broccoli mixture, cheese, pepper, and salt, if desired.

*Makes 2 servings.*

Steve Friedman/Buena Vista Television

*Francis Anthony, the Love Chef, demonstrates his version of tough love along with a delectable banquet.*

# PENNE PASTA WITH PROSCIUTTO SAUCE

Francis Anthony, the Love Chef, travels all over the United States teaching people how to cook. Check out this tasty recipe, which you can easily double. You can use your favorite shape of pasta instead of penne, if you like.

| | |
|---|---|
| 3 | tablespoons butter |
| 4 | ounces prosciutto, cut into ¼-inch-wide strips |
| 1 | small onion, diced |
| 6 | Italian plum tomatoes, diced |
| 1 | cup heavy cream |
| ½ | cup fresh or frozen peas |
| | Freshly ground black pepper to taste |
| ¼ | cup grated Parmesan cheese |
| 8 | ounces penne pasta, cooked according to package directions and drained |

■ In a large skillet, heat the butter over medium heat. Cook the prosciutto and onion for 3 to 5 minutes, or until the onion is tender. Stir in the tomatoes. Add the cream, peas, and pepper and simmer until the mixture is slightly thickened. Add the Parmesan cheese and mix thoroughly. Toss with the pasta.

*Makes 4 servings.*

# BUCATINE CACIO E PEPE

Positano is a sleek Northern Italian restaurant located in the Gramercy Park area of New York City. It is known for its pasta and risotto. Ana Marie Mormando, Positano's general manager, appeared on "Live" to promote the restaurant's upcoming pasta festival. Her segment was entitled "Pasta Mania." After sampling this top-notch dish, you'll understand why!

| | |
|---|---|
| 8 | ounces "straw" or angel-hair pasta |
| 3 | tablespoons olive oil |
| 1 | garlic clove, finely chopped |
| 1 | hot Italian (green frying) pepper, seeded and cut into julienne strips |
| 3 | ounces grated Parmesan cheese |
| 3 | ounces grated Romano cheese |
| 3 | ounces grated provolone cheese |
| 1 | tablespoon cracked black pepper |

■ Bring a large pot of salted water to a boil. Add the pasta and cook just until al dente. Drain thoroughly.

■ In a large skillet, heat the olive oil over medium-high heat. Add the garlic and cook for 2 to 3 minutes, or until lightly browned. Add the pepper strips and cook for 5 to 7 minutes, or until they are just crisp-tender.

▪ Add the pasta, the three cheeses, and the pepper. Toss to coat and serve at once.

*Makes 4 servings.*

# JAMES DARREN'S GRANDMOM'S PASTA

A television star for many years, in "Lost in Space" and "T.J. Hooker," James Darren is also a singer, director, and a spaghetti sauce entrepreneur! James's grandparents came to America from Italy in the early 1900s and his line of sauces is based on recipes that have been in his family for several generations. On "Live," James made this hearty recipe.

| | |
|---|---|
| 10 | ounces Italian sausage (approximately 4 links) |
| 2 | teaspoons water |
| 1 | jar (26 ounces) James Darren Original Family Recipe Pasta Sauce, Basil-Garlic Flavor |
| 1/4 | cup heavy cream |
| 1 | pound rigatoni pasta, cooked according to package directions and drained |
| | Freshly grated Parmesan cheese |

▪ Remove the sausage from its casings and crumble it into a large saucepot. Add the water and cook over low heat for 20 minutes, or until the sausage is cooked. Drain off the fat. Add the pasta sauce and simmer for 5 minutes. Stir in the cream.

▪ Serve the pasta sauce with the cooked pasta and top with Parmesan cheese.

*Makes 6 to 8 servings.*

# *Mostly*
# *Meat*

# STEAK LORENZO

If this flavorful recipe is any indication of stage and screen actor Larry Manetti's culinary prowess, Tom Selleck was lucky to have him as his sidekick on "Magnum P.I." for eight years! As well as being an actor and a producer, Larry has been the co-owner and chef of three restaurants, one with Selleck and one with actor Robert Conrad. This style of recipe comes from the northern part of Italy, where it is a popular way of using leftovers. Larry's particular version, which uses steak, came from his grandmother, and he named it after his son.

On "Live," Larry was red hot—literally. While talking with Regis, he accidentally leaned on the stove and put his hand in the hot skillet and was laughing while he was crying.

| | |
|---|---|
| 2 to 4 | tablespoons olive oil |
| 2 | tablespoons butter |
| 2 | garlic cloves, finely chopped |
| | Fresh or dried rosemary leaves, to taste |
| | Fresh or dried sage leaves, to taste |
| 2 | New York steaks or club steaks (about 1 pound total), cut into bite-size pieces |
| 3 | tablespoons red wine |

■ In a large skillet, heat 2 tablespoons of the oil and the butter over medium-high heat. Add the garlic and cook for 2 to 3 minutes, or until the garlic is lightly browned, stirring constantly. Remove the garlic.

■ Crush the rosemary and sage between your fingertips and add to the skillet. Cook for 1 to 2 minutes, stirring constantly.

■ Season the steak with salt and pepper. Increase the heat to high, add the steak, and cook for 2 to 5 minutes, or until the steak is medium-rare (or the doneness you prefer), stirring constantly.

■ Add the wine, cover, and cook for 1 minute.

*Makes 2 to 4 servings.*

# BLACKENED STEAK

---▪▪---

Meat expert Merle Ellis says there are two things you need to cook blackened meats successfully: a cast-iron skillet and enough fat. While conceding that "fat has become a four-letter word in America," Merle advises that fat is essential for meat to have rich flavor. For a moderate approach, trim off the "waste" (visible) fat and the "taste" fat (the fat that is marbled through the meat) will keep the meat flavorful and tender. Use any leftover seasoning mix from this recipe to add a bit of Cajun flavor to other foods. The mix would add zing to salads and vegetables, too.

| | |
|---|---|
| 2½ | *tablespoons dry mustard* |
| 2 | *tablespoons cayenne pepper* |
| 2 | *tablespoons paprika* |
| 1 | *tablespoon salt* |
| 1 | *tablespoon ground white pepper* |
| 1 | *tablespoon ground black pepper* |
| 1 | *tablespoon ground fennel* |
| 1 | *tablespoon onion powder* |
| 1 | *tablespoon celery salt* |
| 1 | *tablespoon garlic powder* |
| ½ | *cup (1 stick) unsalted butter* |
| | *1-inch-thick steak(s)* |
| | *Sliced tomatoes and onions, for serving (optional)* |

▪ Heat a cast-iron skillet. (The hotter, the better! Keep a fan on or a window open to eliminate any smoke from cooking the meat.)

▪ To make the seasoning mix, combine all of the ingredients except the butter, steak, tomatoes, and onions in a small bowl or covered container.

▪ Melt the butter in a separate pan or in a microwave oven.

▪ Dip the steak in the melted butter, evenly coating both sides. Sprinkle the seasoning mix evenly over both sides. Press the seasoning onto the surface of the steak with your hands. (Save any leftover seasoning mix for other uses.)

▪ To blacken the steak, cook over high heat for about 3 minutes, or until the steak looks charred. Turn the steak over and repeat on the other side. Remove the steak from the pan, lower the heat to medium, return the steak to the pan, and finish cooking the steak until it is done to your taste (about 4 minutes for medium). Drizzle the steak with butter and serve with tomatoes and onions, if desired.

## MERLE ELLIS TELLS HOW TO AGE BEEF

Sometimes people are disappointed with the beef they buy because it has not been properly aged. While aging beef is a simple process, it is expensive because it requires that producers store meat for at least 21 days at 34° to 38° F. Only the top grades of beef—Prime and Choice—can be aged, because they have a substantial layer of fat on the outside that keeps the meat inside from spoiling during the aging process.

Merle Ellis's friend Al Cooper shared with Merle the secret of how to age beef in the refrigerator. Buy a rib-eye or loin strip on sale—either Prime or Choice. Take the meat out of the plastic wrap and rinse it with cold water. Let it drain, then pat it dry with paper towels. Wrap the meat in a large white cotton dish towel and place the package on the bottom shelf of your refrigerator. The next day, unwrap the meat and wrap it in a fresh towel. Continue changing the towel as often as necessary for 10 to 14 days—and you are ready to start enjoying good steaks.

Cut steaks from each end as needed and let the remaining meat continue to age in the refrigerator. Or, if you eat steaks rarely, cut the entire piece of aged meat into steaks, wrap each one in heavy-duty plastic wrap, and freeze until ready to use. Don't forget to label them with the date.

To clean the dishtowels, soak each one as you finish using it in cold water overnight. Next, soak the towels in cold salt water for 2 or 3 hours, and then launder as usual.

# TRADITIONAL MARINATED STEAK BARBECUE

The Clever Cleaver Brothers were dressed in identical striped surfer-boy shirts and started their segment with this rap poem:

> The Cleavers are here to save your day,
> From the big beach buoy in the Maui waves.
> The California studs are on the scene,
> We're dressed to kill, and we're feeling mean.
> We'll show you how—it's not a big deal—
> To make an old-fashioned barbecue meal!

Poem aside, the following recipe is great! (The marinade can be used for chicken and lamb also.)

| | |
|---|---|
| 1 | cup olive oil |
| ½ | cup red wine |
| 1 | garlic clove, finely chopped |
| 1 | tablespoon freshly squeezed lemon juice |
| 1 | tablespoon low-sodium Worcestershire sauce |
| 1 | tablespoon dried oregano leaves or chopped fresh oregano (optional) |
| 2 | pounds skirt steak, trimmed of visible fat |
| | or |
| 2 | pounds chuck steak, trimmed of visible fat |
| | or |
| 2 | pounds tri-tip steak, trimmed of visible fat |
| | Vegetable oil |

▪ In a shallow dish large enough to hold all of the pieces of meat, stir together the oil, wine, garlic powder, lemon juice, Worcestershire sauce, and oregano, if you are using it.

▪ Add the meat. Cover and refrigerate overnight or for at least 3 hours, turning frequently to thoroughly coat the meat.

▪ Using a paper towel, lightly rub a little vegetable oil on the grill or broiler pan. Position this 5 to 6 inches away from the heat source. Pre-heat the grill (or broiler). Cook the meat on both sides until each piece of meat is done to your liking. Baste the meat frequently while you are cooking it. Slice the meat on the diagonal and serve.

*Makes 10 to 12 servings.*

Photo courtesy of The Clever Cleaver Brothers Productions

Et tu, *Regis? The Clever Cleaver Brothers arrive to demonstrate a Caesar salad.*

# Flaming Fajitas

---

Cookbook author Jane Butel specializes in Southwestern-inspired foods that are hot and spicy. In fact, the cookbook she was promoting on "Live" is called *Hotter Than Hell*, which is exactly what happened on the show. The fajitas flamed superbly during the promo, but that made the skillet so hot that the Teflon surface came off and the mixture couldn't sustain a flame! Jane's recipe for fajitas is ideal for entertaining. After flaming the steak (carefully!), keep the meat and tortillas warm and serve them with salsa, chopped onions, sour cream, and guacamole; let your guests "build" their own creations. (You could use the Love Chef's Salsa and Hard Rock "Guac"—see pages 3 and 4.)

| | |
|---|---|
| 1½ | *pounds very lean skirt or bottom round steak, cut ¼ inch thick and trimmed of visible fat* |
| 1 | *lime* |
| 4 | *large garlic cloves, pressed through a garlic press* |
| 1 to 2 | *teaspoons pequin quebrado or crushed red pepper flakes* |
| 2 | *teaspoons vegetable oil* |
| ¼ | *cup brandy* |
| 4 to 6 | *(12-inch) flour tortillas* |
| 4 to 6 | *romaine lettuce leaves, cut crosswise into 1-inch strips* |
| | *Salsa, chopped onions, chopped tomatoes, chopped fresh cilantro, sour cream, and guacamole, for serving with the fajitas, if desired* |

■ Cut the steak into 4 to 6 equal-size rectangles. Pound the steak pieces to flatten them as thin as possible.

■ Cut the lime in half and squeeze the juice over both sides of each piece of steak. Sprinkle the garlic evenly over the steak and then press in the pequin or pepper flakes. Stack the steaks on a plate and let stand for about 30 minutes.

■ Preheat the oven to 250° F.

■ Place a large well-seasoned cast-iron skillet over high heat for about 20 minutes, or until very hot. At the same time, stack the tortillas, wrap in foil, and place in the oven along with 4 to 6 dinner plates. Add the oil to the skillet and quickly sear the meat on both sides.

■ Add the brandy to the hot skillet. Flame the meat by touching the brandy with a lighted match and let the flames burn down. (Keep a large piece of foil or skillet lid nearby in case the flames rise too high. Just cover them until they subside.)

■ Top the warm tortillas with lettuce and pieces of steak. Garnish with salsa, onions, tomatoes, cilantro, sour cream, and guacamole, if desired. To serve, roll each tortilla around the mixture.

*Makes 4 to 6 fajitas.*

---

## DID YOU GET ENGAGED OVER A MEAL?

**KATHIE LEE:** Yes, but who remembers the meal? I wasn't eating. I was in London with Frank, and we went to a very chic restaurant called Annabelle's. They were very, very booked, so they told us, "You'll have to come at eight-thirty." We said "Fine." We arrived at eight-thirty and banged and banged on the door—nobody would let us in. Finally, the maitre d' comes to the door with his jacket off and his tie askew. We look in the back of the place and the waiters are having dinner. We're the only people there! It's not the least bit chic to show up at Annabelle's at eight-thirty.

We went to the bar and spent a long time over a drink, then ordered dinner at ten o'clock. We were still the only people there, except for one person at the bar, and there were violinists serenading us with beautiful music. I started sobbing because Frank had not asked me to marry him, though he'd said that day on the radio he was in London with his fiance. I told him, "I'm not your fiance—you haven't asked me." He laughed, saying, "Well, we will be married." And the violinists played and all the waiters were standing around witnessing me trying to get Frank to ask me to marry him. He finally did, and I finally said "Yes," and I sobbed the rest of the evening, I was so happy. I don't have any idea what I ordered.

# STEAK DIANE WITH COGNAC

Pol Martin, a Canadian food authority, shared this quick and easy recipe with the viewers of "Live." Serve this delectable meat mixture over your favorite type of pasta or rice, and add a tossed green salad to this memorable meal.

| | |
|---|---|
| 2 | tablespoons butter |
| 1¾ | pounds beef tenderloin, thinly sliced |
| | Salt and pepper to taste |
| ¼ | cup cognac |
| 2 | shallots, finely chopped |
| 1 | tablespoon finely chopped parsley |
| 2 | cups brown sauce, heated |
| 1 | tablespoon tomato paste |
| ¼ | teaspoon Worcestershire sauce |
| | Freshly cooked pasta, for serving |

▪ In a large skillet, heat the butter over medium-high heat. Add the steak slices and cook for about 1½ minutes on each side until they are lightly browned. Season with salt and pepper.

▪ Add the cognac. Flame the meat by touching the cognac with a lighted match and let the flame burn down. Remove the meat and reserve.

▪ Add the shallots and parsley to the pan and cook for 2 minutes, stirring frequently. Stir in the brown sauce, tomato paste, and Worcestershire sauce. Bring the mixture to a boil and cook for 2 minutes. Return the meat to the skillet and simmer for several minutes. Serve over pasta.

*Makes 6 servings.*

# CLEVER PIZZAIOLA MEATBALLS

The Clever Cleaver Brothers dressed in full Halloween regalia for this appearance and presented this tasty recipe for meatballs, which is perfect for kids: Each meatball has a surprise stuffing of pepperoni and mozzarella. Even big kids like this recipe!

| | |
|---|---|
| 1 | pound ground beef |
| 1 | large egg white |
| 1/2 | teaspoon dried oregano leaves, crushed |
| 1/2 | teaspoon dried basil leaves, crushed |
| 1/2 | teaspoon garlic powder |
| 1/2 | teaspoon pepper |
| 16 | slices of pepperoni, chopped |
| 1/4 | cup shredded mozzarella cheese |
| | Pasta sauce and freshly cooked pasta, for serving |

▪ Preheat the oven to 350° F.

▪ In a large bowl, combine the ground beef, egg white, oregano, basil, garlic powder, and pepper.

▪ Divide the meat mixture into 8 equal-size portions. Place one-eighth of the pepperoni and one-eighth of the cheese in the center of each portion of meat. Fold the meat over the stuffing mixture and shape it into a meatball.

▪ Place the meatballs in a roasting pan and bake them in the oven for 20 to 25 minutes, or until cooked through. Serve with your favorite sauce and pasta.

*Makes 4 kid-size servings.*

# TACOS À LA MAYOR

Sam Pick, the mayor of the oldest capital city in the United States, Santa Fe, took time off to prepare his specialty for "Live" viewers. This deluxe version of tacos for those who like things hot is a quick recipe for last-minute guests. You can use either ground beef or ground chicken. Look for the seasonings in stores that carry Mexican specialty items.

|       |                                                   |
|-------|---------------------------------------------------|
| 1     | *pound ground beef or chicken*                    |
| 1     | *tablespoon ground pure red chile (mild)*         |
| 1     | *tablespoon ground pure red chile (hot)*          |
| ½     | *teaspoon ground Mexican oregano*                 |
| ½     | *teaspoon ground cumin*                            |
| 1     | *garlic clove, finely chopped*                    |
|       | *Salt to taste*                                   |
| 8     | *taco shells, warmed*                             |
| 1     | *small onion, chopped*                            |
| 2½    | *cups shredded lettuce*                           |
| 1     | *tomato, chopped*                                 |
| 1½    | *cups grated cheese, such as cheddar or Monterey jack* |
|       | *Salsa*                                           |

■ In a large skillet, cook the meat over medium heat for about 5 minutes, or until lightly browned, stirring to break up the meat.

■ Stir in the chiles, oregano, cumin, garlic, and salt. Cook, stirring, for a minute or two longer to allow the flavors to develop. Drain off any fat.

■ Spoon the meat mixture into the taco shells. Top each taco with the onion, lettuce, tomato, and cheese. Spoon salsa over the top.

*Makes 4 servings.*

# Rusty-Burgers

———————■ ■———————

Rusty Staub, former major-league baseball player, broadcaster, and owner of his own restaurant, Rusty Staub's on 5th (at 47th Street) in New York City, appeared on "Live" and prepared his dynamite burgers to celebrate the Fourth of July in 1990. Serve Rusty-Burgers on a bun with lettuce, tomato, and guacamole for a completely satisfying, all-American culinary experience.

| | |
|---|---|
| 1 | tablespoon olive oil |
| 1 | large Spanish onion, finely chopped |
| 1 | large green bell pepper, seeded and finely chopped |
| 2 | pounds ground sirloin |
| 8 | fresh basil leaves, finely chopped |
| 1 | large egg, lightly beaten |
| ½ | cup breadcrumbs |
| | Salt and pepper to taste |

■ In a large skillet, heat the oil over medium-high heat. Cook the onion and pepper for 10 to 12 minutes, or until softened, but not browned.

■ In a large bowl, stir together the beef and the cooked vegetable mixture. Stir in the remaining ingredients until combined. Form the mixture into patties and grill or broil as desired.

*Makes 6 to 8 servings.*

*Regis and chef Marcia Copeland add a little laughter to their recipe.*

# CLASSIC NEW ENGLAND POT ROAST

In honor of the 40th anniversary of the *Betty Crocker Cookbook*, Marcia Copeland from the Betty Crocker Kitchens joined Regis and demonstrated this classic recipe. Marcia reports that while the newest edition of the *Betty Crocker Cookbook* contains the classics, the recipes also strive to "reach to the new." Today's recipes tend to have less salt, less sugar, less fat, and to contain more fresh herbs. According to Marcia, the horseradish is the special ingredient in this recipe, which can be made on top of the stove or in the oven.

    1 to 3   *tablespoons vegetable oil*
        1    *(2-pound) rolled rump roast*
       ½     *teaspoon salt*
       ½     *teaspoon pepper*
       ½     *cup grated horseradish*
About ½      *cup water*
        4    *small potatoes, cut in half*
        4    *medium carrots, cut in half (or use parsnips or rutabagas)*
        4    *small onions, peeled and left whole*

▪ In a Dutch oven or a large heavy saucepot, heat 1 tablespoon of the oil over medium heat.

▪ Cook the meat on all sides until it is browned, adding additional oil if necessary.

▪ Sprinkle the roast with the salt and pepper and spread the horseradish all over the roast. Add ½ cup of water to the pan and cover. Over high heat, bring the water to a boil, then reduce the heat. Keep the pot covered and simmer on top of the stove or bake in a 325° F. oven for 1½ hours. Add the vegetables, cover, and cook for about 1 hour longer, or until the beef and vegetables are tender.

*Makes 4 to 6 servings.*

## TIPS FOR SUCCESSFUL RECIPES

Always read each recipe thoroughly before beginning. Assemble the equipment, prepare the cooking utensils, if necessary, and measure the ingredients.

If necessary, preheat the oven or grill. Check the temperature of your oven with an oven thermometer.

Measure correctly! Be sure to use the appropriate measuring cups for dry and liquid ingredients. Use measuring spoons instead of flatware. Level off dry measures, whether spoons or cups, with the flat edge of a knife or spatula. Read measurements for liquid ingredients at eye level.

# JACK DANIEL'S RIB GLAZE

Lynne Tolley owns Miss Mary Bobo's Boarding House in Lynchburg, Tennessee, an extremely popular place to eat lunch when you visit the distillery of Lynne's great-great-uncle, Jack Daniel. Lynne's Southern-style barbecue sauce has been called "the essence of the spirit of barbecue"; Lynne credits Lynchburg's local product as the reason for its success.

| | |
|---|---|
| 2 | racks of ribs (about 5¼ pounds) |
| | Crushed red pepper flakes to taste |
| 1 | cup Jack Daniel's Whiskey |
| 1 | cup ketchup |
| ½ | cup firmly packed dark brown sugar |
| ¼ | cup vinegar |
| 1 | tablespoon freshly squeezed lemon juice |
| 2 | teaspoons Worcestershire sauce |
| 3 | garlic cloves, finely chopped |
| ½ | teaspoon dry mustard |
| | Salt and pepper to taste |

■ Prepare the grill or broiler.

■ Bring a large pot of water to a boil. Add the ribs and red pepper flakes and boil for about 30 minutes. (This partially cooks the ribs before you barbecue them.)

■ Meanwhile, in a medium saucepan, combine the remaining ingredients and cook over medium heat until the mixture comes to a boil, stirring occasionally.

■ Remove the ribs from the water and place them on the grill. Continually baste the ribs with the sauce and cook them for 15 to 20 minutes, or until they are cooked through. (You can also place the basted ribs in a covered pan and bake them at 350° F. until cooked through.)

*Makes 4 to 6 servings.*

# BARBECUED RIBS EXCALIBUR

Martin Wilk is chef and owner of "Rib Headquarters U.S.A."—the Excalibur restaurant in Southfield, Michigan, a suburb of Detroit. Frank Sinatra, Liza Minnelli, and George Steinbrenner are among the countless fans of Marty's ribs. (In fact, when Frank gets a hankering for Excalibur's ribs, he has them shipped to him!) If you can't get to this Michigan restaurant to sample the ribs in person, try this recipe; it makes a jumbo batch of sauce. Cover and refrigerate any sauce that is left over—you, too, can eat like Frank and Liza.

### BARBECUE SAUCE

|       |                                         |
|-------|-----------------------------------------|
| ¼     | cup corn oil                            |
| 1     | onion, finely chopped                   |
| 1     | tablespoon finely chopped garlic        |
| 1½    | quarts brown stock, heated              |
| ½     | cup red wine vinegar                    |
| ¼     | cup granulated sugar                    |
| ½     | tablespoon dry mustard                  |
| 1     | quart tomato sauce                      |
| 1     | tablespoon liquid smoke                 |
|       | Hot sauce to taste                      |
|       | Mixed barbecue spice to taste (optional)|
| 1     | cup water                               |
| ¾     | cup cornstarch                          |

### RIBS

|   |                                         |
|---|-----------------------------------------|
| 4 | slabs (1¼ pounds each) back pork ribs   |
|   | Garlic salt to taste                    |
|   | Hungarian paprika to taste              |

▪ *To make the sauce:* In a large saucepot, heat the oil over medium-high heat. Add the onion and garlic and cook for 5 to 7 minutes, or until the vegetables are softened slightly.

▪ Add the stock to the saucepot. In a small bowl, stir together the vinegar, sugar, and mustard until the sugar is dissolved. Add this mixture to the saucepot. Stir in the tomato sauce, liquid smoke, hot sauce, and mixed barbecue spice, if desired. Bring the mixture to a simmer and cook for about 5 minutes, stirring frequently.

▪ In a medium bowl, stir together the water and cornstarch until blended. Add the mixture to the saucepot and bring the mixture to a boil. Boil for 1 minute. Remove the pot from the heat. Strain the mixture, if desired.

▪ *To make the ribs:* Preheat the oven to 375° F. Season the ribs with garlic salt and paprika. Place the ribs on a jellyroll pan.

▪ Bake for 30 to 35 minutes. Turn the ribs over and broil for 3 to 5 minutes until crisp on top. Serve the sauce on the side.

*Makes 2 to 4 servings plus leftover sauce.*

*Here's Regis in a tuneful mood.*

Steve Friedman/Buena Vista Television

# ROAST PORK WITH APRICOTS

A native of Germany, Chef Tell was trained in some of the finest restaurants in Europe. Since he arrived in the United States, he has received national recognition because of his frequent television appearances and his innovative yet straightforward recipes. Tell has gone on to produce video cassettes filmed in the Grand Cayman Islands, where he operates a restaurant.

| | |
|---|---|
| 1 | *(2-pound) boneless pork loin roast* |
| 6 to 8 | *dried apricots and/or prunes, pitted* |
| 1 | *medium onion, chopped* |
| 1 | *celery stalk, chopped* |
| 1 | *carrot, chopped* |
| 1 | *cup homemade meat stock or canned chicken broth* |

▪ Preheat the oven to 375° F.

▪ Make a hole in the center of the roast with a sharp knife. Enlarge the hole, using the handle of a wooden spoon.

▪ Fill the cavity with the dried fruit.

▪ Place the meat in a shallow roasting pan and roast for 30 minutes. Add the onion, celery, and carrot to the pan and roast for 20 to 25 minutes longer. Occasionally add stock to the pan and, using a wooden spoon, scrape the pan to loosen the vegetables. (This is called deglazing the pan.)

▪ Remove the pork roast and let stand for 10 minutes before carving. Meanwhile, continue to deglaze the pan with the stock until a sauce has formed. Reheat if necessary. Slice the pork and serve with the vegetable sauce.

*Makes 4 to 6 servings.*

# PORK TENDERLOIN MEDALLIONS WITH GREEN PEPPERCORN SAUCE

When they appeared on "Live" to prepare this recipe, The Clever Cleaver Brothers announced that they had just signed a contract to have a cookbook published. (It's now available by mail order—see page 246.) The green peppercorn sauce provides just the right, intriguing flavor to go with these tender pork medallions. Serve this dish with your favorite fresh vegetables.

| | |
|---|---|
| 12 | 1-inch-thick pieces of pork tenderloin |
| 2 | tablespoons butter |
| 2 | tablespoons olive oil |
| 3 | sprigs of fresh rosemary |
| 3 | garlic cloves, cut into slivers |
| 1/4 | cup Madeira |
| 1/2 | cup heavy cream |
| 2 | tablespoons green peppercorns |
| | Few dashes of aromatic bitters |

▪ Pound each piece of pork until it is about 1/4 inch thick.

▪ In a large skillet, heat the butter and oil over medium-high heat. Add the rosemary and garlic and cook for 30 seconds, stirring constantly.

▪ Add the pork and cook for about 45 seconds on each side. Discard the rosemary and garlic.

▪ Remove the pan from the heat. Carefully add the Madeira and stir to scrape up any browned bits from the bottom of the pan.

▪ Add the cream, peppercorns, and bitters and cook, stirring, over medium heat for 3 to 5 minutes longer, or until the sauce has thickened slightly.

▪ Arrange 3 slices of pork tenderloin on each plate and spoon the sauce over the meat.

*Makes 4 servings.*

*Just clowning around. . . .*

# GYPSY CUTLETS

The singing ringmaster of the Ringling Brothers and Barnum & Bailey Circus, Eric Michael Gillett, can also take center ring in the kitchen. As the big top's train crisscrosses the country, he explains, the members trade and share recipes and cooking secrets with the people they meet. This cutlet recipe is Eric's variation on a dish he learned to make from Magda Saras of the Tokaji Troupe and Anna Jarabek of Norfolk, Virginia. On "Live," Regis donned a tiger-striped tailcoat with mirrored lapels and a sparkling top hat and supervised Eric's preparation of "The Greatest Dish on Earth!"

| | |
|---:|:---|
| 2 | pounds boneless pork chops, cut ½ inch thick and trimmed of visible fat (or veal or chicken, thinly sliced) |
| 1¼ | teaspoons salt |
| 2 | teaspoons ground black pepper |
| 2 to 4 | tablespoons olive oil |
| 3 | garlic cloves, finely chopped |
| 2 | medium onions, sliced |
| 2 | medium tomatoes, cut into quarters |
| ¼ | cup water |
| 1 | teaspoon Worcestershire sauce |
| 2 to 4 | drops of Tabasco |
| | Additional salt and pepper, to taste |

▪ Pound the pork chops to flatten to about ¼ inch thick.

▪ In a small cup, stir together the salt and pepper and sprinkle the mixture evenly over both sides of the cutlets.

▪ In a large skillet, heat 2 tablespoons of the oil over medium-high heat. Cook the cutlets on both sides until they are lightly browned and completely cooked through. Remove the cutlets from the pan; drain and keep them warm.

▪ If necessary, add additional oil to the skillet. Add the garlic and cook for 1 minute. Add the onions and cook for 1 minute. Push the onions to one side of the pan. Add the tomatoes to the other side. Sprinkle with the water, the Worcestershire and Tabasco sauces, and salt and pepper, if desired. Cover the skillet, reduce the heat, and simmer for 5 minutes.

▪ Arrange the cutlets down the center of a warmed platter, with the onions on one side and the tomatoes on the other.

*Makes 4 to 6 servings.*

# STUFFED PORK CHOPS WITH APPLE BUTTER

On The Clever Cleaver Brothers' eleventh appearance on "Live," they presented these pork chops "stuffed for any occasion."

To eliminate some of the work during preparation, it is a good idea to make the apple butter ahead of time and store it in the freezer. Take the cylinder of apple butter out of the freezer about 20 minutes before serving and cut it into slices.

APPLE BUTTER

| | |
|---|---|
| 1 | *medium apple* |
| 1¼ | *teaspoons freshly squeezed lemon juice, divided* |
| ½ | *cup (1 stick) butter, softened* |
| 1 | *teaspoon honey* |
| ¼ | *teaspoon grated nutmeg* |
| ¼ | *teaspoon ground cinnamon* |

## STUFFED PORK CHOPS

| | |
|---|---|
| 4 | thick, boneless center-cut pork chops (each about 6 ounces) |
| 2 | tablespoons butter |
| 2 | tablespoons finely chopped onion |
| 2 | garlic cloves, finely chopped |
| 3/4 | cup raisins |
| 3/4 | cup finely chopped walnuts |
| 1/2 | teaspoon ground allspice |
| | Few dashes of bitters |
| 2 | cups dry bread crumbs |
| 1 1/4 | cups chicken broth, divided |
| 2 | large eggs |

▪ *To make the apple butter:* Core and peel the apple. Place it in a medium saucepan. Add water just to cover the apple. Add 1 teaspoon of the lemon juice. Bring the water to a boil; reduce the heat and simmer for 10 to 20 minutes, or until the apple is soft. Remove the apple from the water and cool completely.

▪ In a medium bowl, combine the apple, butter, honey, nutmeg, cinnamon, and the remaining 1/4 teaspoon of lemon juice.

▪ Spoon the mixture down the center of a piece of plastic wrap. Roll the plastic wrap into a cylinder shape. Label and place in the freezer.

▪ *To cook the pork chops:* Preheat the oven to 350° F.

▪ Using a sharp knife, cut a pocket in each pork chop by slicing it horizontally part of the way through. Place the pork chops in a 13-by-9-inch baking dish.

▪ In a large skillet, melt the butter over medium-high heat. Cook the onion and garlic for 5 to 7 minutes, or until tender. Add the raisins, walnuts, allspice, and bitters and cook until the spices are fragrant, stirring constantly. Remove the skillet from the heat.

▪ In a large bowl, combine the bread crumbs and 1 cup of the chicken broth. Stir in the eggs until blended. Stir in the walnut mixture. Generously fill each pork chop with the stuffing and return them to the baking dish.

▪ Cover the pork chops and bake for about 40 to 50 minutes. Uncover, drizzle with the remaining 1/4 cup of chicken broth, and bake for 5 to 10 minutes longer, or until the chops are lightly browned on top. Top each chop with a slice of apple butter and serve at once.

*Makes 8 servings.*

# LAMB CHOPS IN PARMESAN CRUST

Jeffrey Nathan, owner-chef of the New Deal Restaurant in New York City, prepared this Easter dish, which is the restaurant's most popular menu item. The recipe is far too good to keep for just once a year. You could easily cut it in half to serve at smaller get-togethers.

| | |
|---|---|
| ½ to 1 | cup olive oil |
| 16 | rib lamb chops |
| | All-purpose flour for dredging the chops |
| 6 | large eggs, lightly beaten |
| 1 | pound grated Parmesan cheese |
| ½ | cup (1 stick) butter |
| 2 | medium tomatoes, chopped |
| 8 | garlic cloves, finely chopped |
| 2 | pounds spinach, thoroughly rinsed |
| 1 | teaspoon dried rosemary leaves |
| 1 | teaspoon dried sage leaves |
| | Salt and pepper to taste |
| 2 | lemons, cut into wedges, for garnish |

▪ Preheat the oven to 350° F.

▪ In a large skillet, heat ½ cup of the oil over medium-high heat.

▪ Dip the lamb chops in flour to lightly coat both sides; shake off any excess. Dip the chops in the eggs and then in the Parmesan cheese so that both sides are evenly coated.

▪ A few at a time, cook the chops for about 3 minutes on each side, or until they are lightly browned. Transfer the chops to a roasting pan that is large enough to hold them in a single layer. Bake the chops in the oven for 15 to 20 minutes, or until they are cooked the way you like them (about 15 to 20 minutes for medium-rare).

▪ In another large skillet, heat the butter over medium heat. Add the tomatoes and garlic and cook for 2 minutes, stirring frequently. Add the
spinach and herbs and cook just until the spinach is wilted, stirring frequently. Season with salt and pepper. Serve the lamb chops with the
spinach and garnish with lemon wedges.

*Makes 8 servings.*

# LAMB CHOPS WITH CRACKED PEPPER AND TARRAGON

Michael Roberts was one of the pioneers of California cuisine and his
West Hollywood restaurant, Trumps, is the perfect sunny location for his
creative fare. When he visited "Live," Regis and he got all choked up—
literally—over this fresh-tasting recipe for lamb chops: The heat on the
stove was turned up a little too high, so when Michael seared the chops,
smoke rose—and they were both ready to call the fire department! In
addition to being a successful restaurateur, Michael has published three
cookbooks, *Secret Ingredients*, *Fresh from the Freezer*, and *What's for Dinner?*

| | |
|---|---|
| 1 | tablespoon coarsely crushed black pepper |
| 4 | loin lamb chops |
| 1 | tablespoon olive oil |
| 1/4 | teaspoon salt |
| 1/4 | cup veal stock or canned low-sodium beef broth |
| 2 | tablespoons freshly squeezed lime juice |
| 1 | tablespoon unsalted butter |
| | Grated peel from 1/2 lime |
| 1/2 | tablespoon chopped fresh tarragon or 1/2 teaspoon dried tarragon leaves |

▪ Place the pepper on a plate and press each lamb chop firmly into the
pepper so that it adheres to the meat on both sides.

▪ In a large skillet, heat the oil over high heat. When it is very hot, add the chops and sear quickly on both sides. Sprinkle evenly with the salt and reduce the heat to medium. Add the stock or broth and the lime juice and continue cooking for about 2 minutes, or until done to your taste. Remove the chops and keep them warm.

▪ If you are using dried tarragon, add it to the liquid now. Continue cooking the liquid until it becomes a shiny glaze. Remove the pan from the heat and whisk in the butter. Add the grated lime peel and the fresh tarragon, if you are using it. Spoon the sauce over the chops and serve.

*Makes 2 to 4 servings.*

# Shepherd's Pie

Roy Ackerman is a well-known British food authority and restaurateur, and was the star of the former, and very popular, British cooking show, "The Chef's Apprentice." He prepared this traditional recipe for "Live" viewers. You could use another type of meat or poultry, if you like.

|       |                                                                              |
|-------|------------------------------------------------------------------------------|
| 1     | pound potatoes, peeled and cut into 1-inch pieces                            |
| 2     | tablespoons butter                                                           |
| 3 to 4 | tablespoons milk                                                            |
|       | Salt and pepper to taste                                                     |
| 1     | tablespoon vegetable oil                                                     |
| 2     | small onions, finely chopped                                                 |
| 1     | garlic clove, crushed                                                        |
| 1     | pound lamb, cut into ½-inch pieces, or leftover cooked lamb, ground          |
| ½     | cup lamb or beef stock                                                       |
| ¼     | cup peeled, seeded tomatoes, finely chopped                                  |
| 1     | teaspoon tomato paste                                                        |
| 1     | tablespoon finely chopped fresh mint                                         |

▪ Place the potatoes in a large saucepan. Add enough water to cover. Over high heat, bring the water to a boil. Reduce the heat, cover, and simmer for 15 to 20 minutes, or until the potatoes are tender. Drain the potatoes and reserve.

▪ In a separate pan, melt the butter over medium heat. Add 3 table-spoons of milk and heat through.

▪ In a large bowl, using an electric mixer or a potato masher, beat the potatoes and the butter mixture until smooth. (Add the remaining table-spoon of milk, if necessary, to lighten the potatoes.) Season to taste with salt and pepper and set aside.

▪ Preheat the oven to 425° F. Lightly butter a 9-inch pie plate.

▪ In a large skillet, heat the oil over medium-high heat. Add the onions and garlic and cook for 5 to 7 minutes, or until they are softened.

▪ Add the lamb and cook until browned. Stir in the stock, tomatoes, to-mato paste, mint, salt, and pepper. Transfer the lamb mixture to the pre-pared pie plate. Cover the pie with an even layer of the mashed potatoes. Score the potatoes with a fork. Bake the pie for 20 to 25 minutes, or un-til the filling is bubbling and the potatoes are lightly browned on top.

*Makes 6 servings.*

Steve Friedman/Buena Vista Television

*"You wanna bet?" Kathie Lee is ready to give Regis an earful.*

# LAMB PAPRIKAS

Nora and Jozsef Tolcser of Tigerd, Oregon, were featured on "Live" as winners of the "Be My Valentine" contest. Nora's mother-in-law taught her how to make this delicious version of a classic Hungarian dish that can be served as an everyday meal, yet is sophisticated enough to be offered at a wedding. To complete their "love meal," the Tolcsers add potatoes, a green salad, French bread, and, of course, Hungarian wine.

| | |
|---|---|
| 2 | tablespoons sunflower seed oil |
| ½ | cup chopped onion |
| 3 | pounds leg of lamb, cut into 1-inch cubes |
| 1 | cup chopped green bell pepper |
| 2½ | teaspoons Hungarian paprika |
| 1 | medium tomato, chopped |
| | Salt to taste |
| 2 | cups water |
| ½ | cup all-purpose flour |
| 1¼ | cups sour cream, for garnish |
| | Chopped fresh parsley, for garnish |

▪ In a large saucepot, heat the oil over medium-high heat. Add the onion and cook for 5 to 7 minutes, or until it is translucent. Add the lamb, pepper, and paprika and cook until the lamb is browned on all sides. Add the tomato and salt.

▪ Add the water, reduce the heat to low, cover, and let simmer for 1½ hours, or until the meat is tender, stirring occasionally.

▪ Gradually stir in the flour and cook over medium heat for about 5 minutes, or until thickened, stirring constantly. Top with sour cream and parsley just before serving.

*Makes 8 to 10 servings.*

# Navarin of Lamb

Chef Philippe Boulot, a *Food and Wine* magazine rising star for 1991, is also the creator of Mark's Restaurant at the Mark Hotel in New York City. He shared his delicious recipe for lamb stew with the viewers of "Live." This stew is offered in the restaurant, but Philippe also makes it frequently at home when he has friends over because it creates a "homey ambiance." With it, Philippe serves Côtes du Rhône wine and good bread.

| | |
|---|---|
| 1 | tablespoon vegetable oil |
| 2¼ | pounds lamb shoulder, cut into 1-inch cubes |
| 1 | Spanish onion |
| 1 | tablespoon all-purpose flour |
| 1 | tablespoon tomato paste |
| 1 | garlic clove, crushed |
| 1 | teaspoon dried thyme leaves |
| 1 | teaspoon dried rosemary leaves |
| 1 | bay leaf |
| 4 | cups of freshly cooked root vegetables, such as baby turnips and new potatoes |
| ½ | cup fresh peas |
| | Fresh parsley, thyme, or rosemary, for garnish (optional) |

▪ Preheat the oven to 325° F.

▪ In a Dutch oven or a large heavy saucepot, heat the oil over medium-high heat. Add the lamb cubes and cook until the lamb is browned on all sides.

▪ Add the onion and continue to cook for about 5 minutes longer, or until the onion is slightly softened. Stir in the flour, tomato paste, and enough water to come up to the level of the meat.

▪ Add the garlic, thyme, rosemary, and bay leaf. Cover the pot and bake for about 40 minutes, or until the meat is tender, stirring occasionally. Serve the stew on a warmed serving platter and add the cooked vegetables (heated through, if necessary). Garnish with parsley, thyme, or rosemary, if desired.

*Makes 8 to 10 servings.*

## DOES YOUR DAILY ROUTINE INCLUDE A GOOD MEAL?

**REGIS:** I buy Gelman lunch every day! I get up every morning at seven-thirty, and I'm at the studio by eight-thirty. We wrap up the show at ten. I'm usually in the office the rest of the morning doing interviews, answering fan mail, and attending the production meeting for the next day's show. Then I buy Gelman lunch. Afterward, I'm off to see Boris, my trainer, at Radu's Gym.

# VEAL PARMIGIANA

Ponte's Restaurant in New York City has been considered one of the city's finest Italian restaurants for more than 20 years. On the show, the restaurant's chef, Sabatino Sammarone, shared this recipe for one of his best-loved specialties, Veal Parmigiana. Serve this classic dish with a simple tossed green salad and some crusty Italian bread.

|  | |
|---|---|
| 3 | *large eggs* |
| 1/2 | *cup grated Parmesan cheese, divided* |
| 1 | *tablespoon finely chopped Italian parsley* |
| | *Salt and pepper to taste* |
| 1 | *cup all-purpose flour* |
| 1 | *cup seasoned bread crumbs* |
| 1 | *pound thinly sliced veal cutlets* |
| 1/2 to 1 | *cup olive oil* |
| 4 | *cups tomato sauce* |
| 1/4 | *pound mozzarella cheese, thinly sliced* |

■ Preheat the oven to 550° F.

- In a small bowl, beat together the eggs, 2 tablespoons of the Parmesan cheese, parsley, salt, and pepper. Place the flour and bread crumbs on 2 separate shallow plates.

- In a large skillet, heat about ¼ cup of the oil over medium-high heat.

- Dip each cutlet in the flour to lightly coat both sides; shake off any excess. Dip the cutlets in the egg mixture, and then in the bread crumbs, so that both sides are evenly coated.

- A few at a time, fry the cutlets in the hot oil for about 3 minutes on each side, or until lightly browned. Drain the cutlets on paper towels. Repeat with the remaining cutlets, adding more oil as needed.

- In a 13-by-9-inch baking dish, spread 2 cups of the tomato sauce in an even layer. Arrange the veal cutlets over the tomato sauce. Spoon the remaining 2 cups of sauce over the cutlets. Sprinkle the surface with the remaining 6 tablespoons of Parmesan cheese. Top each cutlet with a slice or two of mozzarella cheese. Bake for 3 to 5 minutes, or until the dish is heated through and the cheese is melted. Serve immediately.

*Makes 4 to 6 servings.*

Steve Friedman/Buena Vista Television

*With a tender morsel perched on his fork, Regis makes a dramatic gesture before sampling his meal.*

# VEAL CASINO

The Love Chef created this easy, sophisticated veal dish that just suits a meal for two! He first introduced the recipe on "Live," and it subsequently won him rave reviews when he cooked it for his first appearance at Trump Plaza Hotel and Casino in Atlantic City, New Jersey.

| | |
|---|---|
| 2 | veal steaks (or chops) |
| | All-purpose flour for dredging the chops |
| 3 | tablespoons olive oil |
| 2 | tablespoons unsalted butter |
| 4 | plum tomatoes, chopped |
| 2 | scallions, chopped |
| 1 | large or 2 small artichoke hearts, sliced |
| 4 | green olives, chopped |
| | Dash of bitters |
| 1/4 | teaspoon dry mustard |
| | Freshly ground black pepper |

▪ Dip the steaks in flour to lightly coat both sides; shake off any excess.

▪ In a large skillet, heat the olive oil and butter over medium heat until the butter is melted.

▪ Cook the steaks for approximately 4 minutes on each side (depending on the thickness of the meat), or until the veal is cooked through. Transfer the steaks to a heated platter and keep warm. Add the remaining ingredients to the skillet and cook for 6 to 8 minutes, or until heated through. Spoon the sauce over the steaks and serve.

*Makes 2 servings.*

# VEAL BIRDS

Chef Tell demonstrated this intriguing recipe in which veal and ham are wrapped around hard-cooked eggs. Try this as an inspired way to use left-over hard-cooked eggs from Easter!

| | |
|---|---|
| 1½ | pounds veal round, cut into ¼-inch-thick slices |
| | Salt and pepper to taste |
| 6 | slices boiled ham |
| 6 | hard-cooked eggs |
| | All-purpose flour, for dredging the veal rolls |
| ¼ | cup (½ stick) butter |
| ½ | cup marsala wine |
| ½ | cup chicken broth |

▪ Preheat the oven to 350° F.

▪ Pound the veal to flatten slightly. Season with salt and pepper.

▪ Place 1 slice of ham and 1 egg on each piece of veal. Roll the veal and ham around the egg and secure the meats around the egg with a tooth-pick. Dip the veal birds in flour to lightly coat; shake off any excess.

▪ In a Dutch oven or large heavy ovenproof saucepot, melt the butter over medium heat. Add the veal birds and cook on all sides, until lightly browned.

▪ Add the marsala and chicken broth to the pot and bake in the oven for 30 minutes.

*Makes 3 to 6 servings.*

*Fowl Play*

# Moghlai Chicken

Madhur Jaffrey, author of some of the best-known and most popular books on Indian and Far Eastern cooking, currently has a PBS television series on those cuisines. She came to "Live" during International Cooking Week and demonstrated this easy recipe for chicken, adapted from her book *A Taste of India*. Moghlai Chicken is a 16th-century dish from the royal courts of the Moghul emperors, and Madhur said it would commonly be served on a banana leaf along with Indian condiments. A couple of days later on the show, Regis commented that Joy had made the dish for him the night before (though not on a leaf), and he thought it was great!

|       |                                                      |
|-------|------------------------------------------------------|
| 1     | *(3½-pound) chicken, cut into pieces*                 |
|       | *Salt and pepper to taste*                           |
| ¼     | *cup vegetable oil*                                  |
| 8     | *whole cloves*                                        |
| 7     | *whole cardamom pods*                                |
| 1     | *2-inch cinnamon stick*                              |
| 2     | *bay leaves*                                          |
| 2½    | *tablespoons blanched, slivered almonds*            |
| 1½    | *tablespoons golden raisins*                         |
| 1     | *cup plain yogurt*                                   |
| 1     | *teaspoon ground cumin*                              |
|       | *Cayenne pepper to taste*                           |

■ Remove the skin from the chicken. Salt and pepper the chicken pieces on both sides.

■ In a large skillet, heat the oil over medium-high heat. When the oil is hot, add the cloves, cardamom pods, cinnamon stick, and bay leaves. (This flavors the oil.) Stir for a few seconds.

■ Add the chicken pieces in a single layer and cook on each side for 3 to 5 minutes, or until lightly browned. Remove the chicken and spices and place them in a bowl. Brown the almonds quickly in the remaining oil.

Stir in the raisins, stir once, and then pour the contents of the skillet into the bowl with the chicken.

▪ In another bowl, stir together the yogurt, cumin, and cayenne pepper until blended.

▪ Pour the mixture over the chicken and toss to coat the pieces.

▪ Transfer the chicken mixture to a large saucepan, cover, and gently simmer over low heat for 20 minutes, turning the pieces of chicken occasionally. Remove the cover, increase the heat, and cook the sauce until it is reduced and thickened. Remove the whole spices before serving.

*Makes 4 to 6 servings.*

# *Y*OGURT *C*HICKEN

Ismail Merchant is the producing half of Merchant-Ivory Productions, which has made so many acclaimed movies, among them *A Room with a View*, *Mr. and Mrs. Bridge*, and *Howard's End*. This successful producer began cooking in 1958 in New York City as a friendly and inexpensive way to gather together the writers, actors, and financiers who were becoming an important part of his business life. His style of cooking is based on his Indian heritage, but he equally easily incorporates French cuisine or the local style of wherever he is. He calls his culinary approach "pragmatic and experimental, and not so different from the way I go about finding financing for my films." *Ismail Merchant's Indian Cuisine*, published in 1986, was the result of his culinary forays.

|  |  |
|---|---|
| ¼ | *cup vegetable oil* |
| 2 | *medium onions, chopped* |
| 2 | *dried whole red chilies, cut in half* |
| 12 | *whole cloves* |
| 2½ | *pounds skinless chicken thighs and drumsticks* |
| 1 | *piece of fresh ginger root (about 1 inch long), peeled and grated* |
| 1½ | *cups plain yogurt* |
| ¼ to ½ | *cup water* |
|  | *Salt and freshly ground black pepper to taste* |

▪ In a large skillet, heat the oil over medium heat. Add the onions and cook for 10 minutes, or until softened, stirring occasionally. Add the chilies and cloves and cook for about 2 minutes.

▪ Add the chicken and ginger and cook for 10 minutes, or until the chicken is lightly browned, stirring frequently. Mix the yogurt with ¼ cup of the water and stir the mixture into the pan. Season with salt and pepper. Cover the skillet and cook over medium-low heat for 1 hour, stirring occasionally. Stir in additional water if necessary. Remove the chilies and cloves before serving.

*Makes 4 to 6 servings.*

# CARIBBEAN-FRIED CHICKEN

"Her name was Lola, she was a showgirl . . ." and Lola Yvonne Bell is one heck of a showgirl when it comes to culinary demos. This New York City restaurateur has starred in a videotape, "Lola's Caribbean-Fried Chicken," and on "Live" she prepared the recipe that follows accompanied by a steel-drum player. Lola, Regis, and the drummer, all dressed in island attire, danced and cooked to the beat. (You could cut the amount of pepper and hot sauce for a milder version.)

1   *(2- to 3-pound) frying chicken, cut into eighths*
1   *lemon, cut in half*
3   *garlic cloves, finely chopped*
3   *tablespoons Hungarian paprika*
2   *tablespoons ground black pepper*
2   *teaspoons salt*
2   *tablespoons dark soy sauce*
2   *tablespoons Louisiana hot sauce*
3   *cups all-purpose flour*
2   *cups vegetable oil*
    *Brown paper bag*

■ Arrange the chicken pieces in a single layer on a plate. Squeeze the lemon over the chicken and store the chicken in the refrigerator for 15 to 30 minutes.

■ Rub the garlic into the chicken and sprinkle the chicken on all sides with the paprika, pepper, and salt. Sprinkle the soy sauce and hot sauce evenly over the chicken.

■ In a large heavy skillet, heat the oil over medium-high heat until hot.

■ Meanwhile, put the flour in the paper bag. Add the chicken pieces and shake until the chicken is coated on all sides; shake off any excess.

■ Place the chicken in the oil and cook the chicken for 10 to 15 minutes on each side until browned and cooked through. Drain the chicken on several layers of paper towels and serve.

*Makes 4 to 6 servings.*

# ROASTED CHILI CHICKEN

Bobby Flay, the chef of the Mesa Grill in New York City, has been called one of the leading experts on Southwestern cuisine in the United States. Look for his book on Southwestern cuisine, which Bobby was working on when he appeared on "Live." Before roasting the chickens for this recipe, Bobby brushed them with a flavorful and fiery seasoned oil. The results are memorable!

| | |
|---|---|
| ½ | *cup peanut oil* |
| 3 | *tablespoons chili powder, divided* |
| 4 | *garlic cloves, peeled and cut in half, divided* |
| 1 | *jalapeño pepper, seeded and chopped* |
| | *Salt and pepper to taste* |
| 2 | *chickens (2½ pounds each) with legs tied together* |
| 2 | *bunches fresh sage or ½ cup dried sage leaves* |
| 2 | *teaspoons red wine vinegar* |
| 1 | *teaspoon prepared mustard* |
| 1 | *teaspoon chopped red onion* |

▪ Preheat the oven to 400° F.

▪ In the container of a food processor fitted with a metal chopping blade, or using a blender, process the oil, 2 tablespoons of the chili powder, 2 of the garlic cloves, the jalapeño, salt, and pepper.

▪ Place the chickens on a rack in the roasting pan. Brush the oil mixture over the chickens. Fill the cavity of each bird with half of the sage and 1 clove of garlic.

▪ Roast the chickens for 50 to 70 minutes, or until they are completely cooked. Remove the sage and garlic and reserve for the sauce. Reserve the drippings and transfer the chickens to a warmed serving platter; keep warm until ready to serve.

▪ In a food processor or blender, process the vinegar, mustard, onion, the remaining 1 tablespoon of chili powder, and the reserved sage and garlic until smooth. Slowly add the pan drippings until the mixture is emulsified. Season with salt and pepper. Slice the chicken and serve with the sauce spooned over the top.

*Makes 8 servings.*

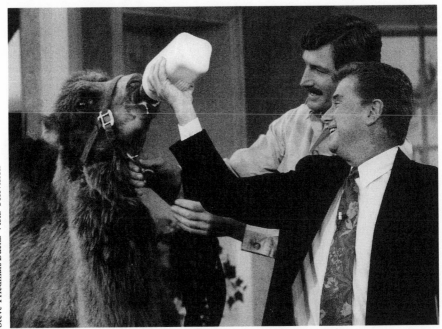

Steve Friedman/Buena Vista Television

**Regis shows animal handler Warren Eckstein and his llama that they have a recipe for just about every guest.**

# BASTILLE DAY CHICKEN

Chef Jean-Louis Gerin of the Restaurant Jean-Louis in Greenwich, Connecticut, prepared this superb chicken dish in honor of Bastille Day, the French national holiday celebrating the fall of the Bastille prison on July 14, 1789. Appropriately, it is his interpretation of a classic 18th-century recipe. Jean-Louis enjoys serving historical recipes in his restaurant, which *USA Today* rated as one of the ten best in the United States. If you can't get to his restaurant, this recipe will help you celebrate the past wherever you live.

|        |                                          |
|--------|------------------------------------------|
| 2      | tablespoons unsalted butter              |
| 4      | chicken thighs                           |
| 3 to 4 | ounces bacon, cut into 1-inch pieces     |
| 24     | pitted green olives                      |
| 4      | anchovy fillets, chopped                 |
| 1      | tablespoon capers                        |
| 1      | teaspoon chopped parsley                 |
| 1      | teaspoon chopped chives                  |
| 1      | teaspoon olive oil                       |
| 1      | cup champagne                            |
| 2      | tablespoons chicken broth                |

▪ In a large skillet, melt the butter over medium-high heat. Add the thighs and cook for 3 to 5 minutes on each side, or until lightly browned. Transfer the thighs to a plate and reserve.

▪ Add the bacon to the skillet and cook for 2 to 4 minutes. Drain off excess fat, if desired. Add the olives, anchovies, capers, parsley, chives, and oil and cook for 5 minutes longer.

▪ Add the champagne and chicken broth and cook for an additional 5 minutes. Return the chicken pieces to the skillet and cook for about 10 minutes, or until the chicken is cooked through.

*Makes 2 to 4 servings.*

# CHICKEN BUNDLES OF LOVE

Sandy Hartley of Springfield, Virginia, won the "Be My Valentine" recipe contest with this sophisticated entry. Her sister, Linda Hofacker, had recently moved to Columbus, Ohio, so Sandy created this change-of-pace dish for their next get-together, minus their children (Sandy has two and Linda has three). The sisters were flown to New York City and reunited on the show.

To complete the adult flavor of the meal, serve it with wild rice and a medley of crisp cauliflower and broccoli florets.

|   |   |
|---|---|
| 4 | boneless, skinless chicken breast halves |
| ¼ | cup almond paste |
| 4 to 6 | ounces mozzarella cheese |
| About ¼ | cup bread crumbs |
| ½ | cup (1 stick) butter |
| 1 | garlic clove, finely chopped |
| ½ | cup sherry |
|   | Pepper to taste |

▪ Preheat the oven to 350° F. Lightly oil a baking dish.

▪ Pound the chicken breasts to flatten them slightly. Spread the almond paste evenly over the breasts. Sprinkle with the cheese and bread crumbs. Roll the chicken over the filling and secure with a toothpick.

▪ In a large skillet, heat the butter over medium-high heat. Add the garlic and cook for 1 minute, stirring constantly. Add the chicken and cook until the pieces are lightly browned, then transfer them to the prepared baking dish. Add the sherry to the skillet, stir until combined, and pour the sauce over the chicken. Bake 20 to 25 minutes.

*Makes 2 to 4 servings.*

# CHICKEN WITH PROSCIUTTO AND CHEESE WITH MUSHROOM SAUCE

Here's just one example of the inspired cuisine served by Chef Jeffrey Nathan from the New Deal Restaurant in New York City. Prosciutto, fontina cheese, and red pepper add moisture and flavor to boneless, skinless chicken breasts.

|     |     |
| --- | --- |
| 2 | large red bell peppers, roasted (see Box) |
| 4 | whole boneless, skinless chicken breasts |
|   | All-purpose flour for dredging the chicken |
| ¼ | cup olive oil |
| ¼ | pound prosciutto, trimmed of visible fat |
| 8 | thin slices of fontina cheese |
| 1 | pound mushrooms, sliced |
| 1 | cup red wine |
| 2 | tablespoons chilled unsalted butter, cut into ½-inch cubes |
|   | Pepper to taste |
|   | Chopped parsley, for garnish (optional) |

## HOW TO ROAST RED PEPPERS

Preheat the broiler. Position a broiler pan so that the tops of the peppers will be about 2 inches away from the heat source. Roast the peppers for about 15 minutes, turning about every 5 minutes, until the skins are blistered and charred. Transfer the peppers to a bowl, cover, and let steam until cooled. Peel the skin from the peppers. Cut each pepper in half lengthwise. Remove the seeds and ribs. Cover and refrigerate.

■ Preheat the oven to 350° F.

■ Lightly pound the chicken breasts to flatten them slightly. Dip the chicken breasts in the flour to lightly coat both sides; shake off any excess.

■ In a large skillet, heat the oil over medium heat. Cook the chicken breasts for about 3 to 5 minutes on each side, or until lightly browned. Transfer the breasts to a baking dish.

■ Top each chicken breast with prosciutto, a red pepper half, and a slice of cheese. Add the mushrooms to the dish. Pour the wine over the chicken and mushrooms. Bake for 20 to 25 minutes, or until the chicken is cooked through and the mushrooms are tender.

■ Transfer the chicken breasts to a warmed serving platter. Using a slotted spoon, remove the mushrooms from the sauce and add them to the platter with the chicken. Keep warm.

■ Pour the sauce from the baking dish into a large skillet and cook over high heat until the liquid is reduced by half. Remove the skillet from the heat. One piece at a time, whisk in the butter. Season the sauce to taste. Pour the sauce over the chicken breasts. Garnish with the chopped parsley, if desired. Serve at once.

*Makes 4 servings.*

*Hey, Reege—ever see a bigger smile?*

# BREAST OF CHICKEN WITH GARDEN VEGETABLES

Chef Luciano Magliulo can cook not only in front of the camera; he used to cook on the rolling seas as a chef on cruise ships. After stints at New York City's Rainbow Room and La Camelia, Luciano is now at home in his own restaurant, Mona Lisa, in Stamford, Connecticut.

This recipe is one that Luciano likes to cook at home on Sundays. He usually keeps a big supply of vegetables on hand and finds this the perfect way to make a one-dish meal.

|       |                                                                                    |
| ----- | ---------------------------------------------------------------------------------- |
| 4     | *chicken breasts*                                                                  |
| 1     | *cup all-purpose flour*                                                            |
| 3     | *tablespoons olive oil, divided*                                                   |
| 1     | *red bell pepper, seeded and sliced*                                               |
| ¼     | *cup sliced mushrooms*                                                             |
| 2     | *tablespoons vegetables cut into julienne strips, such as carrots, celery, and onion* |
| 1     | *tablespoon chopped shallots*                                                       |
| ¼     | *cup tomato sauce*                                                                 |
|       | *Salt and pepper to taste*                                                          |
|       | *Chopped chives, for garnish (optional)*                                            |

▪ Dip the chicken breasts in flour to lightly coat both sides; shake off any excess.

▪ In a large skillet, heat 2 tablespoons of the olive oil over medium-high heat. Add the chicken breasts and cook for 5 to 8 minutes on each side, or until lightly browned. Keep the chicken warm.

▪ In another skillet, heat the remaining 1 tablespoon of olive oil. Cook the pepper, mushrooms, julienned vegetables, and shallots for 3 to 5 minutes, or until slightly softened. Add the tomato sauce and cook for 3 minutes longer. Add the chicken and cook for an additional 5 to 7 minutes, or until the chicken is cooked through. Season with salt and pepper. Garnish with chopped chives, if desired.

*Makes 4 servings.*

# CHICKEN PILAF

When Francis Anthony prepared this delectable dish for "Live" viewers, it's no wonder Regis said, "I love the Love Chef."

| | |
|---|---|
| ⅓ | cup Italian olive oil |
| ⅔ | cup long grain white rice |
| 3 | ounces thin spaghetti, broken |
| 3 | cups chicken broth |
| 1 | cup fresh or frozen broccoli florets |
| ¼ | teaspoon dried thyme leaves, crushed |
| 1 | cup cooked chicken, cut into julienne strips |
| ½ | cup sliced scallions |
| ¼ | cup chopped walnuts |
| ¼ | cup diced red bell pepper |
| | Salt and pepper to taste |

▪ In a large saucepan, heat the oil over medium-high heat. Add the rice and spaghetti and cook for about 5 minutes, or until lightly browned.

▪ Stir in the broth and bring it to a boil. Add the broccoli and thyme. Cover and simmer for 5 minutes. Stir in the chicken, scallions, walnuts, and red pepper. Cover and simmer for 15 minutes, or until tender. Season with salt and pepper.

*Makes 4 servings.*

# SOUTHWESTERN PAN-FRIED CHICKEN

Janos Wilder is one of the leading chefs in the Southwest and the owner since 1983 of the highly esteemed Janos Restaurant in Tucson, Arizona. This recipe combines French cooking techniques with typically Southwestern ingredients.

### CHICKEN

| | |
|---|---|
| 4 | boneless, skinless chicken breast halves |
| 3 | large egg whites |
| 2 | tomatoes, peeled, seeded, and chopped |
| 1 | cup grated cheddar cheese |
| ½ | cup heavy cream |
| 2 | scallions, finely chopped |
| 1 | chili pepper, peeled, seeded, and finely chopped |
| 1 | tablespoon chopped garlic |
| 2 | sprigs of fresh cilantro, finely chopped |
| | Salt and pepper to taste |

### BREADING

| | |
|---|---|
| 1 | cup all-purpose flour |
| 1 | cup milk |
| 4 | cups coarse bread crumbs |
| | Vegetable oil, for frying |
| | Fresh cilantro, for garnish |

▪ Cut the breasts into chunks and process the chicken with the egg whites in a food processor fitted with a metal blade, until just blended.

▪ Place the chicken mixture in a large bowl. Fold in the tomatoes, cheese, cream, scallions, chili pepper, garlic, cilantro, salt, and pepper.

▪ Shape the mixture into 6 patties, each about ½ inch thick.

- Dust each patty with flour, dip into milk, and then coat with the bread crumbs.

- Preheat the oven to 350° F.

- In a large skillet, heat ¼ inch of oil over medium-high heat. Fry each patty for 3 to 5 minutes on each side, or until lightly browned. Place the patties in a baking pan and bake for about 7 minutes, or until cooked through. Garnish with cilantro sprigs and serve immediately.

*Makes 6 servings.*

# MATZOH BALLS WITH CHICKEN

Francine Prince is the queen of healthy cooking and has written ten cookbooks to prove it. She appeared on "Live" to promote the most recent of her books, *Francine Prince's New Jewish Cuisine*, and prepared this special version of matzoh balls. Matzoh balls are dumplings made with matzoh meal instead of flour. Traditionally, they are served at Passover, but they are great at any time of year. Seltzer water gives Francine's matzoh balls a lighter, fluffier texture than usual, and instead of adding them to chicken soup, she recommends serving them in place of potatoes.

| | |
|---|---|
| 2 | *large eggs, separated, plus 1 large egg white* |
| 1 | *tablespoon olive oil* |
| 2 | *teaspoons freshly squeezed lemon juice* |
| ¾ | *pound ground chicken* |
| ½ | *cup finely chopped onion* |
| ¼ | *cup chopped fresh dill or 1½ teaspoon dried dill* |
| ½ | *teaspoon paprika or saffron* |
| ¼ | *teaspoon salt* |
| ¼ | *cup seltzer water* |
| ¾ | *cup matzoh meal* |

*Kathie Lee and her husband, Frank Gifford, sample Francine Prince's special dish.*

▪ In a large bowl, using a fork, stir together the egg yolks, oil, and lemon juice. Stir in the chicken, onion, half of the dill, the paprika or saffron, and salt until thoroughly combined.

▪ Stir in the seltzer. Using a rubber spatula, fold in half of the matzoh meal.

▪ In a large grease-free bowl, beat the egg whites with an electric mixer just until stiff peaks form. Gently fold the whites into the chicken mixture. Sprinkle the remaining matzoh meal over the batter and gently fold it in.

▪ Place the mixture in the freezer for about 30 minutes, or until firm. Shape the mixture into 18 walnut-size balls.

▪ Bring a wide pot of water to a rolling boil. Reduce the heat slightly to a slow boil. Add the remaining dill. Gently ease the matzoh balls into the water. When the liquid begins to simmer, cover the pot and cook for 35 minutes. The matzoh balls will float to the top. Using a slotted spoon, transfer the matzoh balls to hot soup or a warmed serving dish. Serve at once to preserve the texture and shape.

*Makes about 18 matzoh balls.*

**Variation**: This recipe is also excellent made without chicken. If you are using paprika, add an extra ¼ teaspoon. If you are using saffron, the measurement stays the same. The recipe will make 14 to 16 matzoh balls.

# BAKED CHICKEN IN PASTRY

Pano's and Paul's Restaurant is one of the finest dining establishments in Atlanta, Georgia. Its chef, Paul Albrecht, appeared on "Live" to demonstrate this unusual recipe, which has been a favorite ever since it was featured on Pano's and Paul's first menu in 1979. The chicken is baked in a casserole and pastry is wrapped over the actual casserole lid before the chicken goes into the oven.

| | |
|---|---|
| 2 | boneless, skinless chicken breasts, cut in half |
| | Salt and pepper to taste |
| 1/4 | cup butter (preferably clarified) |
| 1 | cup chicken broth |
| 1/2 | cup heavy cream |
| 1 | cup quartered white mushrooms |
| 2 | tablespoons walnut halves |
| 1/4 | cup calvados (apple brandy) |
| 8 | ounces puff pastry or pie dough, rolled out to about 10 inches diameter |
| 1 | large egg, lightly beaten |

▪ Preheat the oven to 375° F.

▪ Season the chicken with salt and pepper.

▪ In a large skillet, heat the butter over medium-high heat. Add the chicken breasts and cook for 2 to 3 minutes on each side, or until lightly browned. Transfer the chicken to a casserole dish that has an ovenproof lid. (It should be no larger than 9 inches in diameter.)

▪ Add the chicken broth and cream to the skillet and stir together. Add the mushrooms and cook over medium-high heat, stirring until the mixture has reduced by about half.

▪ Pour the sauce over the chicken. Distribute the walnuts evenly over the surface. Add the calvados.

▪ Cover the casserole with the lid. Lay the pastry carefully over the top. Glaze with the beaten egg and seal it closed around the edges. Bake for 12 to 14 minutes, or until the pastry is lightly browned.

▪ Carefully cut away the pastry to free the lid. Cut the pastry into pieces and serve it with the chicken mixture.

*Makes 4 servings.*

# TURKEY POT PIE

There's nothing like a pot pie when you are looking for comfort. Pino Piano, the chef from the Mulholland Drive Café in New York City, appeared on "Live" and demonstrated his soul-satisfying version of a turkey pot pie that is covered with puff pastry. This recipe would make great use of leftover Thanksgiving turkey.

| | |
|---|---|
| 4 | *cups chicken broth* |
| 2 | *celery stalks, diced* |
| 1 | *large carrot, diced* |
| 1 | *large red bell pepper, seeded and diced* |
| 8 | *ounces mushrooms, cut into quarters* |
| 1½ | *pounds cooked turkey, cut into bite-size pieces* |
| 5 | *tablespoons butter* |
| 5 | *tablespoons all-purpose flour* |
| ½ | *cup heavy cream, at room temperature* |
| | *Salt, pepper, and Tabasco to taste* |
| 1 | *sheet frozen puff pastry (approximately 10 inches square), thawed according to package directions* |
| 1 | *large egg, lightly beaten* |

▪ In a large skillet, combine the chicken broth, celery, carrot, and pepper and bring the mixture to a boil over high heat. Add the mushrooms and simmer until the vegetables are tender.

▪ Strain the broth into a large bowl. Place the vegetables in a 10-inch pie plate or quiche dish. Stir in the turkey.

▪ In the same skillet, melt the butter over medium heat. Add the flour and stir until smooth and bubbly; cook for 2 minutes, stirring constantly. Gradually add the hot chicken broth, stirring after each addition. Increase the heat to medium-high and cook until the mixture boils and thickens, stirring constantly, for about 5 minutes. Add the cream and continue cooking until thickened.

▪ Season the sauce with salt, pepper, and Tabasco. Pour the sauce into the plate with the vegetables and turkey and stir to combine. Refrigerate the filling until completely cooled.

▪ Preheat the oven to 350° F.

▪ On a lightly floured surface, using a rolling pin, roll out the sheet of puff pastry until it is about 12 inches square. Cut an 11½-inch circle out of the dough and lay it over the filling, pressing the edges to the rim of the container. Lightly brush the crust with the beaten egg. Using the point of a small sharp knife, cut several holes in the top of the crust. Bake the pot pie for 20 to 25 minutes, or until the filling is bubbly.

*Makes 6 to 8 servings.*

## WHAT ARE YOUR FAVORITE FOODS?

**REGIS:** "Now, don't write this down. I like a slice of white bread that's topped with a thinly sliced cheese like mozzarella or Monterey jack. Put it under the broiler until the cheese melts and top it with a couple of sliced tomatoes—and that's it. You know what else I like? Don't write this down, either. A Ritz cracker spread with a little peanut butter and then just a little bit of strawberry jam—only strawberry jam, don't give me raspberry or any other flavor, just strawberry jam. Also: coffee ice cream, Oreos, bread and butter, beef barley soup, hamburgers, grilled chicken sandwiches from the ABC cafeteria with fried onions and tomato, bacon and eggs (when Gelman isn't on the cholesterol patrol), cheese enchiladas, Harvest Crisp crackers, and, in Oriental restaurants, orange crispy beef."

**KATHIE LEE:** "Pasta, bananas, cherries, potatoes, and corn."

# GRILLED CHICKEN WITH WATERMELON PICO DE GALLO

The Mansion on Turtle Creek Hotel and Restaurant in Dallas, Texas, has been singled out as one of the best in the world, and Dean Fearing, its charming chef, has received national acclaim for his cooking. This fresh-tasting recipe is just one example of Dean's innovative Southwestern cuisine. Try this at your next outdoor barbecue. Make sure the Pico de Gallo ingredients are cut into ¼-inch cubes so that the flavors really have a chance to intermingle.

### WATERMELON PICO DE GALLO

| | |
|---|---|
| 1½ | cups diced watermelon |
| ½ | cup diced jicama |
| ½ | cup chopped fresh cilantro leaves |
| ¼ | cup diced honeydew melon |
| ¼ | cup diced cantaloupe |
| ¼ | cup diced red onion |
| 2 | tablespoons freshly squeezed lime juice |
| 1 | fresh jalapeño pepper, seeded and finely chopped |
| ½ | teaspoon salt (or to taste) |

### GRILLED CHICKEN

| | |
|---|---|
| 2 | tablespoons peanut oil |
| 4 | whole boneless, skinless chicken breasts |
| | Salt and freshly ground black pepper to taste |

▪ In a large bowl, gently toss all the Watermelon Pico de Gallo ingredients to combine. (Try not to break up the watermelon pieces.)

▪ Using a paper towel, lightly rub a little peanut oil on the grill or the broiler pan. Position the grill or broiler 5 to 6 inches away from the heat source. Brush the chicken with the remaining oil and season with salt and pepper. Grill or broil the chicken for 5 to 7 minutes on each side, or until cooked through. Serve immediately with the Watermelon Pico de Gallo.

*Makes 4 servings.*

# GRILLED CHICKEN WITH FRUIT

Chef Katsuo Sugiura (Suki) from the Grand Café at the Grand Bay Hotel in Miami was one of the principal chefs involved in the SOS (Share Our Strength) Taste of the Nation fundraiser that took place in Miami in 1989. When Chef Suki came to "Live" to re-create this refreshingly tropical chicken dish, he somehow got lost in the ABC studios and made it to the set just seconds before going on the air. Fortunately, he had prepared the marinade ahead of time—and so should you.

| | |
|---|---|
| 1/2 | cup vegetable oil, plus extra for oiling the grill |
| 1/4 | cup chopped onion |
| 2 | tablespoons finely chopped garlic |
| 1/2 | cup freshly squeezed lemon juice, divided |
| 1 | tablespoon dried oregano leaves |
| 4 | boneless, skinless chicken breasts (6 ounces each) |
| 1/2 | cup freshly squeezed orange juice |
| 1/4 | cup red wine vinegar |
| 1/3 | cup diced papaya |
| 1/3 | cup diced mango |
| 2 | tablespoons chopped Italian parsley |

▪ In a large skillet, heat the oil over medium-high heat. Add the onion and cook for 5 to 7 minutes, or until the onion is translucent. Add the garlic and cook for about 2 to 3 minutes longer, or until the garlic is tender. Stir in 1/4 cup of the lemon juice and the oregano. Cool the mixture slightly. Toss the chicken breasts with the marinade, cover, and refrigerate for 4 to 5 hours.

▪ Remove the chicken from the marinade. Using a paper towel, lightly rub a little vegetable oil on the grill or broiler pan. Position this 5 to 6 inches away from the heat source. Preheat the grill (or broiler). Cook the chicken breasts for 5 to 7 minutes on each side, or until cooked through.

▪ In a medium bowl, combine the remaining ¼ cup lemon juice, the orange juice, vinegar, papaya, mango, and parsley. Serve the sauce with the chicken.

*Makes 4 servings.*

# JAMAICAN JERK RUB

Helen Willinsky started her culinary career at the age of 13 in Kingston, Jamaica, where she baked pies and cakes for her parents' friends. Now she has written a cookbook, *Barbecue from Jamaica*, and runs a company called Helen's Tropical Exotics that makes a number of island-inspired products, one of which is jerk rub. Jerk is a spicy, tangy way of marinating and cooking that Jamaicans have used for 300 years, and that Helen has helped popularize in America. On the show, she prepared the following recipe with Regis chiming in with an occasional "Day-o!" (To simplify this process you can mail-order Helen's jerk products—see page 246.)

|  |  |
|--:|:--|
| 1 | onion, finely chopped |
| ½ | cup finely chopped scallions |
| 2 | teaspoons fresh thyme leaves |
| 2 | teaspoons salt |
| 1 | teaspoon ground Jamaican pimiento |
| ½ | teaspoon ground cinnamon |
| ¼ | teaspoon grated nutmeg |
| 4 to 6 | finely chopped hot peppers (such as Jamaican Scotch bonnets) |
| 1 | teaspoon ground black pepper |
| 4 | large chicken breasts (or 2 racks of pork ribs or 1 large fish) Vegetable oil, for oiling the grill |

- In a large bowl, mix together all of the ingredients except the chicken and the oil to make the jerk rub.

- Smear the chicken breasts all over with the jerk rub and place the breasts in a buttered glass baking dish. Cover and let stand for 2 to 3 hours or overnight. (Let the ribs stand for the same amount of time, but cook the fish immediately.)

- Preheat the oven to 275° F. Bake the chicken for 30 minutes.

- Using a paper towel, lightly rub a little vegetable oil on the grill or broiler pan. Position it 5 to 6 inches away from the heat source. Preheat the grill (or broiler). Place the chicken breasts with the skin sides facing the heat source and grill or broil for 5 minutes on each side, or until the skin is crispy and the chicken is cooked through.

*Makes 4 servings.*

# PREHISTORIC BARBECUED CHICKEN

The Clever Cleaver Brothers were at it again with this recipe for barbecued chicken caveman style! Clad in animal skins, Lee Gerovitz and Steve Cassarino showed how to satisfy the most primeval appetite. You can use whatever chicken pieces you like best—white or dark meat.

| | |
|---|---|
| 4 | *pieces of chicken* |
| 1/2 | *cup low-sodium Angostura soy sauce* |
| 1/2 | *cup grape juice* |
| 1 | *tablespoon firmly packed brown sugar* |
| 1/2 | *tablespoon vegetable oil* |
| 1/2 | *teaspoon grated fresh ginger root* |
| 1/4 | *teaspoon finely chopped garlic* |
| | *Vegetable oil* |

## Clever Barbecue Tips from The Clever Cleaver Brothers

**1.** If you are making kebabs, soak wooden skewers for at least 1 hour before you are ready to use them. This will keep them from burning on the grill.

**2.** When you use traditional charcoal on your grill, stack the charcoal so that it forms a pyramid. Soak the charcoal with lighter fluid. When the coals absorb the lighter fluid, ignite carefully. After the coals turn gray, spread them evenly. They are now ready for cooking.

**3.** For additional flavor when you are grilling, try using hickory and/or mesquite chips that have been soaked in water for at least 1 hour. Just before you are ready to cook, sprinkle some of the soaked wood chips on the gray coals. When the chips begin to smoke, they will impart their delicious aroma to the food you are cooking. (If you don't soak the chips, they will just burn away, not smolder as they should.)

**4.** To impart a sweet flavor to your food, instead of soaking your hickory or mesquite chips in water, use Angostura aromatic bitters. Put some of your wood chips in a clean jar (such as a mayonnaise jar). Pour in enough bitters to cover the chips. Set aside to let the wood soak for a couple of days, then use them as you would other soaked wood chips.

▪ Remove the skin from the chicken and submerge the pieces in boiling water for 15 minutes.

▪ In a large bowl, stir together the remaining ingredients to make the sauce. Add the chicken pieces, cover, and refrigerate for 30 minutes, or until ready to cook.

▪ Using a paper towel, lightly rub a little vegetable oil on the grill or broiler pan. Position this 5 to 6 inches away from the heat source. Cook the chicken for 5 to 7 minutes on each side, or until cooked through, brushing the chicken occasionally with the sauce.

*Makes 2 to 4 servings.*

# CHICKEN PICKUP STICKS

Rich Davis, cookbook author and creator of K.C. Masterpiece Barbecue Sauce, demonstrated this recipe for tasty kebabs that are low in calories and fat. The day that Rich appeared on the show, he did his demonstration on the street corner in front of the WABC studios. During the segment, people who walked by kept saying, "Why, that looks like Regis Philbin!"

| | |
|---|---|
| 1 | cup barbecue sauce |
| ¼ | cup chopped fresh cilantro |
| 3 | tablespoons soy sauce |
| 2 | tablespoons white vinegar |
| 2 | tablespoons Oriental sesame oil |
| 1 | pound boneless, skinless chicken breasts, cut into 2-inch pieces |
| 1 | large onion, cut into 1-inch pieces |
| 1 | large green bell pepper, cut into 1-inch pieces |
| 12 | cherry tomatoes |
| 1 | small zucchini, cut into 1-inch-thick slices |
| | Vegetable oil |
| | Freshly cooked rice |

▪ In a small bowl, stir together the barbecue sauce, cilantro, soy sauce, vinegar, and sesame oil. Place the chicken, onion, green pepper, tomatoes, and zucchini in a large heavy-duty plastic bag. Add the barbecue sauce mixture, seal the bag tightly, and let the mixture marinate in the refrigerator for 6 hours.

▪ Remove the bag from the refrigerator. Alternate the chicken and vegetables on 4 skewers. Reserve the marinade.

▪ Using a paper towel, lightly rub a little vegetable oil on the grill or broiler pan. Position this 5 to 6 inches from the heat source. Preheat the grill (or broiler). Cook the kebabs for 2 to 4 minutes on each side, basting occasionally with the reserved marinade. Serve the kebabs with rice.

*Makes 4 servings.*

# CHAPTER 6

# *Under the Sea*

# SHRIMP SAMANTHA WITH ANDOUILLE

When the executive chef of Brennan's, Michael J. Roussel, prepared this Louisiana-style recipe for "Live," he had to make two extra batches because it was so popular with the crew and cameramen. Brennan's is probably the most renowned restaurant in that city of great eating, New Orleans. This dish is named after the daughter of the restaurant's owner, Jimmy Brennan. If you like, you can use less garlic than Michael does.

| | |
|---|---|
| ½ | cup (1 stick) butter |
| 1 | cup sliced fresh mushrooms |
| ½ | cup chopped white onions |
| ½ | cup chopped scallions |
| ¼ | cup finely chopped garlic |
| 2 | pounds peeled fresh shrimp |
| 1 | pound andouille sausage or spicy smoked sausage, cut into bite-size pieces |
| ½ | cup dry white wine |
| | Freshly cooked rice, for serving |

- In a large skillet, melt the butter over medium-high heat.

- Cook the mushrooms, onions, scallions, and garlic. Cook for 3 to 4 minutes, or until the vegetables are softened but not browned. Add the shrimp and sausage and cook about 4 minutes longer. Add the wine and simmer briefly until everything is cooked through. Serve over rice.

*Makes 8 servings.*

## WHAT IS IT LIKE EATING WITH CODY?

**KATHIE LEE:** Cody sits at the table with us. When we say grace, he's the one who gets to say "Amen." He knows when I pause that it's time to say, "Aaaamen!" Of course, he's already eaten about six bites. I haven't taught him yet that he's not supposed to eat during the prayer.

# GRILLED SHRIMP SALAD WITH GINGER

Award-winning chef Vincent Guerithault visited "Live" and demonstrated this special salad recipe, in which strips of tortilla add textural interest. He serves this unique medley at his restaurant, Vincent Guerithault, on Camelback in Phoenix.

½   cup plus 2 tablespoons olive oil
2   tablespoons sherry wine vinegar
2   tablespoons fresh basil leaves, chopped
1   tablespoon diced red bell pepper
1   tablespoon diced green bell pepper
1   tablespoon fresh ginger root, cut into julienne strips
2   corn tortillas, cut into ½-inch strips
1   tablespoon diced tomato
    About 4 cups of an assortment of lettuce leaves
    Salt and pepper to taste
    Vegetable oil
1   pound large shrimp, peeled

▪ In a medium skillet, heat the olive oil until it is warm. In a large bowl, combine ½ cup of the warm olive oil with the vinegar, basil, peppers, and ginger.

■ Heat the remaining 2 tablespoons of oil over medium-high heat. Add the tortillas and cook until lightly golden. Using a slotted spoon, remove the tortillas from the skillet. Add the tortillas, tomatoes, and lettuce greens to the large bowl and toss to combine. Season with salt and pepper.

■ Using a paper towel, lightly rub a little vegetable oil on the grill or broiler pan. Position this 5 to 6 inches away from the heat source. Preheat the grill (or broiler). Brush the shrimp lightly with the remaining oil in the skillet. Cook the shrimp for about 30 to 60 seconds on each side, or until cooked through.

■ Arrange the salad mixture on a plate, top with the hot shrimp, and serve.

*Makes 4 servings.*

# GRANDMA CECILIA'S "SHRIMP ON FIRE"

Restaurateur Lola Yvonne Bell, who is of Jamaican descent, was the first featured chef during International Cooking Week in March 1992. She and Regis did a reggae dance as they prepared this Caribbean recipe on "Live." Plain cooked rice provides the ideal balance for the spicy shrimp mixture, and an island-style beverage would be the perfect cooler.

| | |
|---|---|
| 1½ | pounds shrimp |
| 8 | tomatoes |
| 4 | tablespoons olive oil, divided |
| 1 | cup cognac |
| 1 | cup chopped shallots |
| ½ | cup chopped celery |
| 2 to 3 | garlic cloves, finely chopped |
| 1 | teaspoon cayenne pepper |
| | Freshly cooked rice |

■ Peel and devein the shrimp. To devein the shrimp, using the point of a sharp knife, make a shallow cut down the center back (the curved side) of each shrimp and remove the dark vein. Rinse away any bits of the vein that remain.

■ Submerge the tomatoes in boiling water for 30 seconds. Place in cold water and remove the skins and cores. Dice the tomatoes.

■ In a large skillet, heat 2 tablespoons of the oil over medium-high heat. Add the shrimp and cook for 4 to 6 minutes, or until heated through, stirring frequently.

■ Add the cognac to the skillet. Flame the shrimp by touching the brandy with a lighted match and let the flame burn down. Using a slotted spoon, remove the shrimp from the skillet and reserve.

■ In the same skillet, heat the remaining 2 tablespoons of the olive oil. Add the shallots, celery, and garlic and cook for 5 to 7 minutes, or until the vegetables are softened.

■ Stir in the tomatoes and cayenne pepper. Cook over low heat for about 20 minutes, or until the tomatoes have started to soften and form a sauce, stirring occasionally.

■ Return the shrimp to the skillet and heat through. Serve over rice.

*Makes 4 to 6 servings.*

# *B*AY *S*TATE *W*IGGLE

The Moosewood Restaurant in Ithaca, New York, has been famous for its inspired cuisine with a healthful, vegetarian emphasis ever since its opening in 1973. The restaurant is collectively owned and operated, and one of its members, Maureen Vivino, appeared on "Live" to demonstrate this appealing recipe from the restaurant's latest cookbook, *Sundays at Moosewood Restaurant.* Sunday nights at Moosewood are different from the rest of the week because on Sundays the collective's members "stretch" and experiment with one particular ethnic or regional cuisine. Inspiration for Bay State Wiggle comes from Massachusetts' cuisine, which combines old English dishes with fresh seafood and creamy sauces.

Serve this recipe as a supper entrée, along with a light, brothy soup such as an onion soup and a crisp salad of fresh greens and marinated carrots in a simple vinaigrette. It also makes an excellent brunch dish. You could accompany it with your favorite dry white wine or champagne.

1    *pound medium shrimp*

1    *pound fresh asparagus, cut into bite-size pieces*

4    *tablespoons butter, divided*

¼    *cup unbleached all-purpose flour*

2    *cups milk, heated*

     *Salt and freshly ground black pepper to taste*

2    *tablespoons dry white wine*

     *Toasted French or Italian bread, rice, biscuits, or egg noodles*

     *Hungarian paprika, for garnish*

4    *sprigs of fresh dill, for garnish*

▪ Peel and devein the shrimp. To devein the shrimp, using the point of a sharp knife, make a shallow cut down the center back (the curved side) of each shrimp and remove the dark vein. Rinse away any bits of the vein that remain.

▪ In a steamer basket over boiling water, lightly steam the asparagus for 3 to 4 minutes, or until it is just tender. Drain and set aside.

▪ In a large saucepan over medium heat, cook 3 tablespoons of the butter until melted. Whisk in the flour and cook over low heat for 1 to 2 minutes, stirring constantly. While stirring, gradually add the hot milk. Continue to cook and stir for about 5 minutes, or until the sauce thickens. Season with salt and pepper.

▪ In a skillet, cook the remaining 1 tablespoon of butter over medium heat. Add the shrimp and cook for 2 to 4 minutes, or just until they begin to turn pink. Stir in the wine and cook for about 2 minutes. Using a slotted spoon, remove the shrimp from the cooking liquid and keep warm. Stir the shrimp cooking liquid into the white sauce. If the sauce is too thin, set the pan over medium heat and let it cook for 1 to 3 minutes, or until it thickens.

▪ Arrange the toast, rice, biscuits, or noodles on each plate. Top with the shrimp and asparagus and then spoon the sauce over the dish. Garnish each plate with a sprinkle of paprika and a sprig of fresh dill.

*Makes 4 servings.*

# GINGER SHRIMP

Canadian Pol Martin is both a celebrity chef and a cookbook author. His cookbook, *Easy Cooking for Today*, is filled with quickly made recipes like this Oriental-style dish that is delicious served over rice.

| | |
|---|---|
| 1 | tablespoon vegetable oil |
| 1½ | pounds medium shrimp, peeled and deveined |
| | Salt and pepper to taste |
| 1 | red bell pepper, seeded and thinly sliced |
| 1 | celery stalk, thinly sliced |
| 1 | carrot, peeled amd thinly sliced |
| 3 | scallions, cut into ¾-inch pieces |
| 2 | tablespoons finely chopped fresh ginger root |
| 1½ | cups chicken broth, heated |
| 2 | tablespoons cold water |
| 1 | tablespoon cornstarch |

▪ In a large skillet or wok, heat the oil over high heat. Cook the shrimp for 4 to 6 minutes, or until cooked through, stirring frequently. Season with salt and pepper. Remove the shrimp and reserve.

▪ Add the red pepper, celery, carrot, scallions, and ginger root to the skillet and cook for 3 to 4 minutes, or until the vegetables are just starting to soften, stirring constantly.

▪ Add the chicken broth and bring to a boil. In a small cup, stir together the water and cornstarch until blended, then stir into the vegetable mixture.

▪ Return the shrimp to the skillet and cook until the mixture comes to a boil. Cook for 1 minute longer, or until the sauce thickens.

*Makes 4 servings.*

# SCALLOPS WITH TOMATO SAFFRON SAUCE

This is just one of the inventive recipes that Jeffrey Nathan serves at the New Deal Restaurant in New York City. Alison Nathan, his wife and former assistant, revealed that though Jeffrey appears calm and collected on "Live," he is actually a nervous wreck from the time he is booked until he appears on the show.

Jeffrey likes to use Gem scallops in this dish. At the time of the show, these delicate scallops had just been discovered in the waters off New Zealand, at depths hundreds of feet lower than where scallops are usually found.

| | |
|---|---|
| ¼ | teaspoon saffron |
| ¼ | cup cognac |
| 3 | large leeks |
| 1 | tablespoon unsalted butter |
| 2 | ripe tomatoes, cut into ½-inch pieces |
| 1½ | tablespoons diced shallots |
| 20 | Gem scallops in their shells or 1½ pounds sea scallops in their shells, thoroughly scrubbed |
| 1 | cup white wine |
| ½ | cup heavy cream |
| | Salt and pepper to taste |
| | Freshly cooked rice pilaf, brown rice, or Basmati rice, for serving |

∎ In a small cup or bowl, add the saffron to the cognac and allow it to sit for 10 minutes; stir. (The cognac should turn to a golden-red color.)

∎ Trim off the base and the tough green leaves of the leeks and discard, leaving about a 4-inch piece of the tender part of each leek. Cut the leeks into julienne strips and rinse thoroughly.

▪ In a large skillet, heat the butter over medium-high heat. Add the leeks, tomatoes, and shallots. Cook for 4 to 6 minutes, or until the leeks are translucent.

▪ Add the scallops, white wine, and saffron-cognac mixture. Cover the pan and steam for about 4 minutes, or until the scallops' shells open or they are cooked through.

▪ Add the heavy cream and bring the mixture back to a boil. Reduce the heat to a simmer. Using a slotted spoon, remove the scallops from the pan and place them on 4 warmed pasta plates. Continue simmering the sauce for 1 to 2 minutes, or until the sauce is slightly thickened. Season with salt and pepper. Spoon the sauce over the scallops. Serve immediately with a rice dish such as rice pilaf, brown rice, or Basmati rice.

*Makes 4 servings.*

# SMOKED ORIENTAL SEAFOOD

The River Club's head chef, Jeff Tunks, appeared on "Live" to demonstrate a signature recipe from this establishment in Washington, D.C., which *Esquire* magazine proclaimed one of the best new restaurants in 1988. Jeff likes to add an Asian influence when he cooks, which is evident in this easy, effective dish. This recipe would go nicely with rice.

| | |
|---|---|
| 2 | tablespoons finely chopped fresh ginger root |
| 2 | tablespoons finely chopped garlic |
| 1 | tablespoon hot sauce |
| ½ | cup olive oil |
| 2 | pounds of any shellfish |
| 1 | bunch scallions, finely chopped |
| ½ | cup soy sauce |

▪ In a small bowl, make a paste of the ginger, garlic, and hot sauce and reserve.

- In a wok or large skillet, heat the oil over high heat until it is almost smoking.

- Add the shellfish and cook for 2 minutes, stirring constantly with a wooden spoon. Stir in the paste and the scallions and cook 1 minute longer, stirring constantly. Add the soy sauce and scrape up any browned bits from the bottom. Serve immediately.

*Makes 6 to 8 servings.*

# LEMON CRUMB-BAKED COD

To quote Kathie Lee, "Francis Anthony, affectionately known as the Love Chef, has become a regular favorite on our show. He is full of enthusiasm, wit, and best of all, great recipes." This quick, flavorful recipe is just one of them. Make sure to grate the lemon peel before you squeeze the lemons for juice, and when you grate them, take care not to grate below the zest (the yellow part of the peel), because the white part tastes bitter.

| | |
|---|---|
| 1 | cup unseasoned dry bread crumbs |
| 1/2 | cup freshly squeezed lemon juice |
| 2 | tablespoons butter, melted |
| 2 | tablespoons olive oil |
| 1 | tablespoon finely chopped parsley |
| 1 | tablespoon finely grated lemon peel |
| 1/2 | teaspoon paprika |
| 1/8 | teaspoon ground white pepper |
| 1 1/2 | pounds cod fillets |

- Preheat the oven to 350° F.

- In a medium bowl, stir together all of the ingredients except the fish.

- Place the fish fillets in a baking dish and spread the bread crumb mixture evenly over the fish. Bake for 20 minutes, or until the fish flakes easily when touched with the tines of a fork.

*Makes 4 servings.*

## WHAT FOOD DO YOU LOVE, NO MATTER WHAT?

**KATHIE LEE:** Most of my childhood we lived near the Chesapeake Bay, so I have great memories of crab feasts, which would go on for two days. We'd order bushels and bushels of crabs and cook them ourselves, season them, and eat them off newspapers spread on the tables. You'd have to bathe in lemon juice afterward, because you smelled so horrible, but it was worth it. I hate to get messy, so Frank can't believe that I really don't mind sitting down at a table full of disgusting crabs. I'll ruin a good manicure before I'll turn down a crab.

# SEASONED RICE SEAFOOD SALAD

Cooking wizard Chef Paul Prudhomme of the esteemed New Orleans restaurant, K-Paul's Louisiana Kitchen, has frequently brought his Louisiana cuisine to "Live." The following recipe would be excellent for a summertime meal.

| | |
|---|---|
| 1 | quart water |
| | Juice of 1 medium-size lemon |
| 4 | tablespoons Chef Paul Prudhomme's Seafood Magic®, divided |
| 4 | (6 ounces each) drum or other firm-fleshed fish fillets |
| 1 | cup canned crushed tomatoes |
| ½ | cup white vinegar |
| ¼ | cup chopped dill pickle |
| 1 | cup vegetable oil |
| 6 | cups cooked rice |
| 1 | cup chopped onion |
| 1 | cup chopped celery |
| ½ | cup chopped green bell pepper |
| | Lettuce leaves, for serving |

▪ Over high heat, in a 10-inch skillet, heat the water, lemon juice, and 1 tablespoon of the Seafood Magic for about 8 to 9 minutes, or until the mixture comes to a hard simmer.

▪ Gently place 2 fish fillets in the bottom of the skillet and cook for about 4 minutes, or until the fish changes from translucent to an opaque milky white and feels firm.

▪ Using a slotted spoon, carefully remove the fish and set aside. Repeat the procedure with the remaining fish. Refrigerate the fish to cool.

▪ In a large bowl, thoroughly combine the tomatoes, the remaining 3 tablespoons of Seafood Magic, vinegar, and dill pickle. Whisking constantly, gradually stream the oil into the mixture until it is all incorporated and the dressing is thick. Stir in the rice, onion, celery, and bell pepper and mix until combined.

▪ Remove the cooled fish from the refrigerator and carefully break the fillets into bite-size pieces. Carefully fold the pieces of fish into the salad.

▪ Place a lettuce leaf on each of 6 serving plates. Mold about 1⅔ cups of salad in the center of each lettuce leaf.

*Makes 6 servings.*

Steve Friedman/Buena Vista Television

*Offstage antics mesmerize the hosts.*

# Irish Salmon with Cucumber Sauce

Who better to visit "Live" on St. Patrick's Day than a chef from the Emerald Isle? Elma Campion is chef at the spectacular 15th-century Dromoland Castle, which once belonged to the royal O'Brien family and now is a princely hotel that offers meals fit for kings and queens.

Elma selected this traditional Irish recipe because the green cucumber sauce on a white plate with the golden salmon echoes the colors of Ireland's flag—and because some of the best salmon in the world is caught off Ireland's west coast. (If you cannot find salmon, however, Elma suggests substituting cod or halibut.) After her demonstration, though, Regis mistakenly sampled the half-cooked salmon instead of the finished dish Elma had ready. The chef blamed it on the mischievous spirits haunting Dromoland Castle!

> 2 *large tomatoes*
> 2 *large cucumbers*
> 1/4 *cup water*
> 2 *tablespoons unsalted butter*
> *Salt and freshly ground pepper to taste*
> 1/4 *cup vegetable oil*
> 4 *fresh salmon fillets without skin or bones*
> *Juice of 1 lemon*
> *Chopped fresh chives, for garnish*

■ Preheat the oven to 350° F.

■ Submerge the tomatoes in boiling water for 30 seconds. Place in cold water and remove the skins and cores. Dice the tomatoes.

■ Peel and seed the cucumbers. Using a melon baller, scoop the flesh into balls, reserving the scraps.

Steve Friedman/Buena Vista Television

**_Elma Campion treats Regis to salmon with a green cucumber sauce on St. Patty's day._**

▪ In a saucepan, combine the water, butter, cucumber scraps, salt, and pepper. Cover, and cook over low heat for 2 to 3 minutes.

▪ In a large skillet, heat the oil over medium-high heat. Add the salmon and cook for 2 to 3 minutes, or until the salmon is seared on both sides. Bake the salmon in the oven for 4 minutes, or until cooked to the doneness you prefer.

▪ Add the lemon juice to the cooked cucumber mixture and process the mixture in a food processor or blender until smooth.

▪ Divide the sauce among 4 plates and spread it into a thin pool on each one. Place a salmon fillet in the center of each plate. Garnish with the chopped tomato, cucumber balls, and chopped chives.

*Makes 4 servings.*

---

## WHAT MEALS WERE MOST MEMORABLE?

**REGIS:** "The flounder at Le Cirque is pretty tough to beat and so is the Dover sole at La Grenouille."

**KATHIE LEE:** "Every meal Frank and I ate on our cruise to Monte Carlo and up the northern coast of Italy was great! We'd stop at little out-of-the-way Italian restaurants and we loved the local food."

---

# SAUMON AVEC COULIN D'AVOCAT (SALMON WITH AVOCADO SAUCE)

Chef Georges Perrier is often rated as one of the top chefs in the United States. This is one of his favorite recipes from his distinguished restaurant, Le Bec Fin, in Philadelphia. It is easy, elegant, and impressive.

| | |
|---|---|
| 1 | ripe avocado, pitted and peeled |
| 1 | cup chicken broth |
| 1 | tablespoon sherry vinegar |
| About ½ | cup heavy cream |
| | Salt and pepper to taste |
| 1 | pound salmon, cut into 4 fillets |

▪ In the container of a food processor fitted with the metal blade, process the avocado, chicken broth, ½ cup of cream, salt, and pepper until smooth. Add additional cream, if necessary, to thin the sauce. Strain the sauce into a saucepan.

▪ Heat the sauce over medium heat, stirring frequently. *Do not allow it to boil!*

- In a large non-stick skillet, cook the salmon for 3 to 5 minutes, or until lightly browned and cooked through.

- Divide the sauce among 4 plates and spread it into a pool on each one. Place a salmon fillet in the center of each plate.

*Makes 4 servings.*

# PAN-SEARED SALMON WITH ZUCCHINI, SPINACH, AND BROCCOLI

Marcel Desaulniers is the witty and charming chef of The Trellis Restaurant in Williamsburg, Virginia. He selected this recipe because it is appealing to the eye and very easy to prepare. Marcel used a chef's *mandoline*—a flat-bladed cutter—to cut the zucchini, but if you don't have one, you can coarsely shred the zucchini in a food processor. The day Marcel was on the show, his own segment went off smoothly, but he was upstaged in the next segment by a puppy that got fresh with Kathie Lee and flipped up her skirt.

| | |
|---|---|
| 4 | *pounds zucchini, washed and lightly peeled* |
| 2½ | *pounds broccoli* |
| 4 | *cups loosely packed spinach leaves with stems removed* |
| 4 | *tablespoons olive oil* |
| 8 | *4-ounce salmon fillets* |
| | *Salt and pepper to taste* |

- Prepare the vegetables. Using a mandoline, cut the zucchini into thin spaghetti-like strands the length of the zucchini and about ⅛ inch wide. Remove the stems from the broccoli and cut the broccoli into florets. Cut the spinach into ¼-inch-wide strips.

▪ Bring a pot of salted water to a boil for the broccoli.

▪ In each of 2 large skillets, heat 2 tablespoons of the olive oil over medium-high heat. When the skillets are hot, place the zucchini and spinach in one pan and the salmon fillets in the other. Season with salt and pepper. Cook the vegetables for about 5 minutes, or until hot. Sear the salmon for 1½ to 2 minutes on each side.

▪ Cook the broccoli florets in the boiling water for 2½ to 3 minutes, or until tender but still crunchy.

▪ Make a 1½-inch-wide ring of zucchini and spinach around the outer edge of each of 8 warmed 9- to 10-inch pasta plates. Arrange the broccoli florets in a ring, stem ends toward the center, inside the zucchini ring. Place a salmon fillet in the center of each ring of broccoli and serve immediately.

*Makes 8 servings.*

*Kathie Lee and Michael Gelman discuss business while Regis checks the set one last time.*

Steve Friedman/Buena Vista Television

# WARM TUNA SALAD

New Deal chef Jeffrey Nathan brought this delectable dish to the viewers of "Live" from his restaurant in New York City. This recipe gives tuna salad a whole new meaning! Jeffrey likes to serve the tuna medium-rare.

| | |
|---|---|
| ½ | cup extra-virgin olive oil, divided |
| 2 | 6-ounce tuna steaks |
| | Salt and pepper to taste |
| | Cracked black pepper to taste |
| 2 | bunches arugula, rinsed well |
| 2 | heads Belgian endive, leaves separated or chopped |
| 1 | head radicchio, leaves separated and rinsed well |
| 2 | tomatoes, diced |
| 1 | cucumber, thinly sliced |
| ½ | cup black olives |
| 1 | medium red bell pepper, seeded and diced |
| 1 | medium yellow bell pepper, seeded and diced |
| 1 | tablespoon balsamic vinegar |

■ In a large skillet, heat ¼ cup of the oil over medium-high heat. Season the tuna steaks with salt, pepper, and cracked black pepper. Cook the tuna steaks for 2 to 4 minutes on each side, or until the tuna is seared on each side, but not cooked through. It should be medium-rare.

■ In a large bowl, toss together the arugula, endive, radicchio, tomatoes, cucumber, olives, red pepper, and yellow pepper. Divide this mixture between two large plates.

■ Slice the tuna against the grain and arrange the slices on the salad.

■ In a small bowl, mix together the remaining ¼ cup of olive oil and the balsamic vinegar and ladle this mixture over the salad. Serve at once.

*Makes 2 servings.*

# BEER BATTER FISH AND SPICY DIPPING SAUCE

You might not recognize Joel Rapp when he's in the kitchen wearing an apron because you usually see him in his Mr. Mother Earth sweatshirt giving tips on gardening. Joel was on the show promoting his cookbook *Fabulous Fish*, and this recipe certainly fits that category. Joel was on in the last segment of the show when there were only three minutes left, but somehow he managed to complete this dish in that amount of time with stellar results. Serve the fish with—what else?—french fries and coleslaw.

### BEER BATTER

| | |
|---|---|
| 1 | cup all-purpose flour |
| 1 | teaspoon cornstarch |
| | Salt and pepper to taste |
| 2 | eggs, separated |
| 2 | cups beer |
| 2 | tablespoons vegetable oil |

### SPICY DIPPING SAUCE

| | |
|---|---|
| ½ | cup ketchup |
| 1 | tablespoon hot red salsa sauce |
| 2 | tablespoons grapefruit juice |
| 1 | tablespoon lime juice |
| 1 | tablespoon Worcestershire sauce |
| 1 | tablespoon prepared horseradish |
| | Dash of Tabasco |

### FISH

| | |
|---|---|
| 1 to 2 | pounds of fish such as cod fillets, shrimp, or scallops |
| | Vegetable oil, for frying fish |

■ *To make the batter:* In a large bowl, stir together the flour, cornstarch, salt, and pepper. Stir in the egg yolks until combined. Stir in the beer and the oil. Cover and refrigerate for 3 to 12 hours. Reserve the 2 remaining egg whites in the refrigerator.

■ *To make the sauce:* In a medium bowl, stir together all of the dipping sauce ingredients until combined.

■ Just before serving, in a large grease-free bowl, beat the egg whites with an electric mixer until soft peaks start to form. Fold the whites into the beer batter.

■ Pour oil into a deep-fat fryer or a heavy saucepan and heat to 375° F. Dip each piece of fish in turn into the batter and fry until golden brown and cooked through. Drain on paper towels. Serve with the sauce.

*Makes 4 to 8 servings.*

# FISH WITH PUFF SAUCE

Earl "Butch" Fullmer prepared this specialty from his restaurant, the Red Cedar Inn in McGregor, Iowa. Butch has the longest handlebar mustache in McGregor—and probably in New York City, too! Regis usually just tastes the recipes prepared on the show, but he liked this fish dish so much that he ate his whole serving—at about 9:30 A.M., too. Whether you offer it for breakfast or dinner, this easy preparation is one you will want to use again and again.

Butch suggests serving the fish with broiled grapefruit halves. Slice grapefruits in half. Cut carefully around each section to loosen. Dot the top of each half with butter and then sprinkle with brown sugar. Place the grapefruit halves under the broiler and broil until the tops are bubbly.

2  pounds firm fish fillets
   Salt to taste
1  tablespoon olive oil or melted butter
2  tablespoons lemon juice, divided
½  cup mayonnaise
2  tablespoons sweet pickle relish, drained
2  tablespoons finely chopped fresh cilantro or parsley
   Cayenne pepper to taste
2  large egg whites, at room temperature

- Preheat the oven to 450° F. Lightly oil a baking sheet.

- Arrange the fish fillets on the prepared baking sheet. Season with salt, if desired. Brush the fish with olive oil or butter and drizzle 1 tablespoon of the lemon juice over the fish. Bake the fish for 10 to 15 minutes or until almost cooked through. (The time will depend on the thickness of the fish.)

- While the fish is baking, make the sauce. In a medium bowl, stir together the mayonnaise, pickle relish, cilantro, the remaining tablespoon of lemon juice, salt, and cayenne pepper. In a large grease-free bowl, beat the egg whites with an electric mixer until stiff peaks start to form. Fold the whites into the mayonnaise mixture until just combined.

- Spread the sauce over each fish fillet. Return the fish fillets to the oven and bake 5 minutes longer, or until the sauce is puffed and golden brown. Serve at once.

*Makes 6 servings.*

## How Adventurous Are You about Eating?

**JOY PHILBIN:** Over the years, Regis has become much more adventurous and will eat just about anything except a mushroom. His mother was a very good cook who preferred very basic but hearty dishes, and she never used a recipe. Her Italian dinners were Regis's favorites. When we were first married, I would experiment every night and try out a different recipe, and every night Regis would say, "This looks scary—can't we just have spaghetti?"

# SALMON FILLETS WITH CRISPY SKIN

Chef André Soltner of the highly esteemed Lutèce in New York City made this unique variation of salmon. Salmon fillets take on a whole new look with diagonal slashes across them. Then this innovative chef serves the fillets atop a salad made from tender lettuce leaves.

|       |                                                     |
|-------|-----------------------------------------------------|
| 4     | 3- to 4-ounce boneless salmon fillets with the skin on |
| 4     | tablespoons vegetable oil, divided                  |
| 2     | shallots, finely chopped                            |
| ½     | ounce of finely chopped fresh herbs                 |
| 1½    | tablespoons balsamic vinegar                        |
| ½     | teaspoon coarse salt                                |
|       | Freshly ground pepper to taste                      |
| ½     | pound tender lettuce, torn into bite-size pieces    |

▪ Preheat the oven to 350° F.

▪ With the point of a sharp knife, make diagonal slashes spaced ½ inch apart on the skin of each fillet. Repeat, going in the opposite direction to create a cross-hatch pattern.

▪ In a large skillet with an ovenproof handle, heat ½ tablespoon of the oil over medium-high heat. Add the salmon fillets, skin side down, and cook for 5 minutes. Place the skillet in the oven and bake for 1 to 3 minutes longer, or until heated through.

▪ In a large bowl, stir together the remaining 3½ tablespoons of oil, the shallots, herbs, vinegar, salt, and pepper. Toss with the lettuce leaves. Arrange the lettuce leaves on individual plates and top each plate with a salmon fillet placed skin side up.

*Makes 4 servings.*

# Seafood Shish Kebab

During barbecue week at "Live," Jeffrey Nathan prepared these irresistible kebabs with a flavorful hot and spicy dipping sauce that will appeal to seafood lovers. The New Deal chef recommends serving these kebabs with Basmati rice or a lobster risotto.

### Tequila-Lime Marinade

- 1/4 cup tequila
- Juice from 2 limes
- 1 tablespoon chopped fresh cilantro
- 1 teaspoon finely chopped fresh herbs
- Salt and pepper to taste

### Seafood Kebabs

- 1/2 pound salmon fillets, cut into 1-inch cubes
- 1/2 pound tuna fillets, cut into 1-inch cubes
- 1/2 pound medium shrimp, peeled and deveined
- 1/2 pound swordfish, cut into 1-inch cubes
- 2 onions, cut into 1-inch pieces
- 2 red peppers, seeded and cut into 1-inch pieces
- 2 yellow peppers, seeded and cut into 1-inch pieces
- Vegetable oil, for oiling the grill

### Hot and Honey Sauce

- 1/2 cup hot sauce (such as Louisiana Red Hot Sauce)
- 1/4 cup honey
- 3 tablespoons butter, melted
- 1 tablespoon white vinegar
- 1 teaspoon Tabasco
- 1 teaspoon finely chopped garlic
- 1/4 teaspoon celery salt

▪ *To make the marinade:* In a shallow glass dish large enough to hold 8 kebabs, combine the marinade ingredients. Thread the kebab ingredients alternately onto 8 skewers and place the kebabs in the marinade. Cover and refrigerate the kebabs for 2 hours before cooking, turning them frequently.

▪ *To make the sauce:* Stir together all the sauce ingredients.

▪ *To make the kebabs:* Using a paper towel, lightly rub a little vegetable oil on the grill or broiler pan. Position this 5 to 6 inches away from the heat source, then preheat the grill (or broiler). Remove the kebabs from the marinade and arrange on the hot surface. Cook the skewers for 5 to 7 minutes, or until the kebabs are cooked through, turning them frequently. Serve the kebabs with the dipping sauce.

*Makes 8 servings.*

# *L*OLA'S *Q*UICK *R*ED *S*NAPPER

Restaurateur Lola Yvonne Bell specializes in spicy, stylish Caribbean cuisine. When she isn't in the kitchen, Lola is busy studying decorators' and designers' plans for an exciting new Manhattan restaurant.

| | |
|---|---|
| 1 | large tomato, peeled and chopped |
| 2 | scallions, chopped (including the tender green tops) |
| 1 | garlic clove, finely chopped |
| 2 | teaspoons Louisiana hot sauce |
| 1 | sprig fresh thyme or ½ teaspoon dried thyme leaves |
| ½ | teaspoon salt |
| ⅓ | cup olive oil |
| ¼ | cup (½ stick) butter |
| 2 | red snapper fillets (about 1½ pounds) |
| 1 | lemon, cut in half |

■ In a small bowl, stir together the tomato, scallions, garlic, hot sauce, thyme, and salt.

■ In a large skillet, heat the olive oil and butter over medium heat until the butter melts.

■ Place the fish in the skillet. Squeeze the lemon over the fillets in the pan. Spoon the tomato mixture evenly over the fish, cover the skillet tightly, and cook for 10 minutes. (Check with a spatula to make sure that the fish is not sticking to the bottom of the skillet.) Reduce the heat and simmer for about 10 minutes longer, or just until the fish is cooked through. (Use a fork to test whether the fish is cooked through and tender.)

*Makes 4 servings.*

# Santa Barbara Surfer's Sauté

Johnny Ciao comes from the world of rock-and-roll cuisine and has cooked for many stars, among them Marlon Brando, Gregory Peck, Michael Jackson, and Whitney Houston. Before Johnny cooks anything, he likes to add a little music. On the show, he played his harmonica over the top of the ingredients used in the recipe that follows and presented Regis with a harmonica so that he would be able to play for Joy at home. Johnny believes that cooking is like music because you are actually composing as you cook. In this dish, for instance, he calls the garlic and onion "the bottom end," the peppers "the rhythm track," the capers "the string section," and the squash "the lead guitar." Shaking the pan, of course, is "the mix." Accompany your composition with freshly cooked rice or pasta.

| | |
|---|---|
| ¼ | *cup olive oil* |
| ½ | *onion, chopped (preferably a Maui onion)* |
| 1 | *garlic clove, finely chopped* |
| 1 | *red bell pepper, chopped* |
| 1 | *Anaheim chili or green bell pepper, finely chopped* |
| 1 | *teaspoon capers* |
| 1 | *medium tomato, chopped* |
| 1 | *medium yellow squash or zucchini, chopped* |
| 6 to 8 | *fresh basil leaves, torn* |
| 1 | *pound whitefish fillets* |
| | *Freshly cooked rice or pasta, for serving* |

▪ In a large skillet, heat the oil over medium-high heat. Add the onion and garlic and cook for 3 to 5 minutes, or until lightly golden.

▪ Add the red pepper, the chili or green pepper, and the capers and cook for 30 seconds. Add the tomato, squash, and basil leaves and toss in the pan for 1 minute.

▪ Place the whitefish on top of the vegetables. Cover the pan, reduce the heat to low, and cook for 2 to 3 minutes, or until the fish is just cooked through and opaque.

*Makes 2 to 4 servings.*

## HOW DO YOU WORK MEALS INTO YOUR BUSY SCHEDULE?

**KATHIE LEE:** I get up around 6:20 and throw on a sweat suit and jump in the car. I have a cup of tea and a SlimFast bar while I'm driving into the city. From seven-thirty to nine, I get my hair washed and styled, then I get my makeup. At the same time, I'm briefed by the producers and read the information I need for that day's show. The show is over at ten o'clock. Sometimes we have post-tapes or commercials to shoot, but my favorite kind of day is when I can go home and be with my little boy Cody. I love to take him out so he can have pizza.

# *S*NAPPER *C*APRICE

Chef Tell's Grand Old House in the Cayman Islands features distinctive Caribbean cuisine. Chef Tell Erhardt appeared on "Live" and prepared one of his restaurant's most popular dishes, Snapper Caprice. The delicious tropical chutney can also be served over roast chicken, Cornish game hens, and roast turkey.

|     |     |
| --- | --- |
| 1 | *cup diced onions* |
| 1 | *cup diced peeled apples* |
| 1 | *cup diced bananas* |
| 1 | *cup diced mangoes or peaches* |
| ½ | *cup raisins* |
| ¼ | *cup plus 2 tablespoons white wine, divided* |
| ¼ | *cup vegetable oil* |
| ¼ | *cup red wine vinegar* |
| 1 | *teaspoon granulated sugar* |
| ½ | *teaspoon dried thyme leaves* |
|   | *Salt and pepper to taste* |
| 1 | *pound boneless snapper fillet* |
| 2 | *tablespoons all-purpose flour* |
| 1 | *tablespoon olive oil* |

▪ In a large saucepan, combine the onions, apples, bananas, mangoes, raisins, ¼ cup of the white wine, vegetable oil, vinegar, sugar, thyme, salt, and pepper. Cook over low heat for about 1 hour, stirring occasionally. Cool completely.

▪ Dip the fish in the flour to lightly coat both sides; shake off any excess.

▪ In a large skillet, heat the oil over medium-high heat. Add the fish and cook for 3 to 5 minutes on each side, or until cooked through and lightly browned. Remove the fish to a plate and keep warm. Drain off the liquid from the skillet. Add the remaining 2 tablespoons of wine and the chutney to the pan and heat through. Serve the chutney over the fish.

*Makes 2 to 4 servings.*

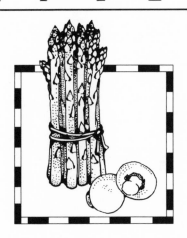

# *On the Side*

# PERFECT SOUTHWESTERN POTATO SALAD

This delicious and flavorful salad was prepared by Bobby Flay, executive chef of New York City's Mesa Grill. It would be good with Bobby's Roasted Chili Chicken (page 90).

| | |
|---|---|
| 12 | *new potatoes (about 2 pounds), thoroughly scrubbed* |
| | *Salt and pepper to taste* |
| 1½ | *cups mayonnaise* |
| 1 | *tablespoon Dijon-style mustard* |
| | *Juice of 1 lime* |
| 1 | *medium tomato, chopped* |
| ½ | *medium red onion, chopped* |
| 2 | *scallions, chopped* |
| 2 | *tablespoons chopped fresh cilantro* |
| ½ | *medium jalapeño pepper, seeded and finely chopped* |
| 1 | *small garlic clove, finely chopped* |
| ½ | *teaspoon cayenne pepper* |

▪ In a large saucepan, bring to a boil enough salted water to cover the potatoes. Add the potatoes and cook for 20 to 30 minutes, or until the potatoes "give" slightly when stuck with the point of a sharp knife. Drain the potatoes and cut into ¼-inch-thick slices.

▪ Meanwhile, in a large bowl, stir together the remaining ingredients. Add the warm potato slices and toss gently to coat. Cover and refrigerate to blend the flavors.

*Makes 4 to 6 servings.*

# KILLER MASHED POTATOES

These aren't just any old mashed potatoes! These are potatoes with pizzazz, created with love by Francis Anthony, the Love Chef. Garlic aficionados can substitute finely chopped fresh garlic for the garlic powder—either raw or cooked with the scallions.

| | |
|---|---|
| 4 | large potatoes, thoroughly scrubbed |
| ¼ | cup (½ stick) butter |
| 1 | small bunch scallions, sliced |
| 1 | tablespoon grated fresh horseradish or prepared horseradish |
| 1 | teaspoon garlic powder |
| 2 | tablespoons grated Parmesan cheese |
| ½ | cup milk (or more if necessary) |
| | Salt and freshly ground pepper to taste |

▪ Trim off any "eyes" or discolored spots from the potatoes. Cut the potatoes into quarters.

▪ In a large saucepan, cook the potatoes in boiling salted water for 20 to 30 minutes, or until soft. Drain the potatoes.

▪ In a large saucepan, melt the butter over medium heat. Cook the scallions for 3 to 5 minutes, or until they are softened but not browned.

▪ Add the scallion mixture and the remaining ingredients to the potatoes. Using a potato masher, mash the potatoes to a slightly lumpy consistency. Keep the potatoes warm in an ovenproof container in a warm oven until ready to serve.

▪ If you like, you can make this dish a day ahead. After mashing the potatoes, put them in a bowl, cover, and refrigerate. Reheat the mashed potatoes thoroughly in the microwave or in a warm oven before serving.

*Makes 4 to 6 servings.*

# Spoon Bread

The late Helen Dickerson appeared on "Live" on her 80th birthday, when she made this traditional, simple Southern dish—and sang to Regis! Originally from the South, Helen worked at Cape May, New Jersey's oldest hotel, The Chalfonte, for more than 40 years. The title of her book aptly describes the preparation of spoon bread (and many more of Helen's recipes): *I Just Quit Stirrin' When the Tastin's Good*. Good advice—and a delicious recipe.

| | |
|---|---|
| 1 | cup white or yellow cornmeal |
| ¼ | cup all-purpose flour |
| 1 | tablespoon baking powder |
| 1 | teaspoon salt |
| ½ | cup water |
| 2 | tablespoons lightly salted butter |
| 2 | cups evaporated milk |
| 3 | large eggs, beaten |

▪ Preheat the oven to 450° F. Generously butter a 2-quart casserole dish.

▪ In a large bowl, stir together the cornmeal, flour, baking powder, and salt. In a small saucepan, combine the water and butter. Cook over high heat until it comes to a boil. Pour the water mixture over the cornmeal mixture and stir until blended. (The mixture will be dry.) Stir in the milk and eggs and beat until smooth. (The batter will be very thin.)

▪ Pour the batter into the prepared dish. Bake for 20 to 25 minutes, or until a toothpick inserted into the center comes out clean. Serve immediately.

*Makes 8 servings.*

# GARLIC RICE WITH PINE NUTS

There was plenty of "play" on the set when Steve Sax, second baseman for the Chicago White Sox, demonstrated this high-carbohydrate, low-fat rice dish. Regis and Steve kept tossing the ball back and forth over the countertop, and it was debatable whether there would actually be any food prepared or not. Of course, Steve can catch, and he made sure Regis didn't "strike out" the glass dish of rice. When you prepare the rice for this recipe, try using chicken broth in place of the water. You can serve this colorful dish with fish or chicken.

| | |
|---|---|
| 1 | tablespoon butter or margarine |
| ¼ | cup pine nuts or slivered almonds |
| 1 | small red bell pepper, seeded and cut into thin strips |
| 1 | small green bell pepper, seeded and cut into thin strips |
| 1 | garlic clove, finely minced |
| 2 | cups freshly cooked rice |
| 2 | tablespoons chopped fresh parsley |

▪ In a large skillet, heat the butter over medium-high heat. Cook the pine nuts for 1 to 2 minutes until lightly golden, stirring constantly.

▪ Add the pepper strips and garlic and cook for 5 to 7 minutes, or until the peppers are tender. Stir in the cooked rice and the parsley and heat for 2 to 3 minutes, or until heated through.

*Makes 4 servings.*

*Too many cooks can spoil the broth.*

*All dressed up and no place to go? Regis and Kathie Lee's formal attire bedazzles the audience.*

*Kathie Lee and Joy brew up some trouble for Regis.*

*Mark and Jessica Vanase are thrilled about their Valentine's Day wedding, celebrated with Regis and Kathie Lee.*

Steve Friedman/Buena Vista Television

*Cheers! Here's to another fun-filled hour with America's most popular morning-TV team.*

*Kathie Lee makes sure Regis tries Tommy Tang's new recipe.*

*Cody makes his dancing debut with Mom, Kathie Lee, on Mother's Day.*

*Sportin' more than a wee bit o' green on St. Patrick's day, Kathie Lee proves she's no late bloomer.*

**Regis and Kathie Lee share a tender moment.**

**The Trinity Irish Dancers perform a traditional dance, and Regis and Kathie Lee, in the St. Patrick's Day spirit, do a jig along with them.**

**"Look, Ma—no hands!"**

*Regis and Kathie Lee look skeptical, but Chef Tell assures them his summertime spread is positively delectable.*

*Regis flaunts the latest media splash.*

*With their stockings hung by the chimney with care, Regis and Kathie Lee settle down to a favorite Christmas story.*

*Christmas time is family time. From left to right: Frank Gifford and Cody with Kathie Lee. After Santa are daughters Joanna and Jennifer Philbin with Regis and Joy. Santa is played by the youngest son of the Douglas dynasty, Eric Douglas, a guest on that morning's show.*

# RIVERBANK BARBECUE BAKED BEANS

Sportscaster Curt Gowdy was right at home in the woodsy environment (complete with tent!) created for him on the stage at "Live." Curt, the host of ABC's "American Sportsman" for 20 years, is an avid fisherman and outdoorsman. He was on the show to promote Neiman Marcus's *Pure & Simple Cookbook*. As his fashion statement, Regis sported a bandana neckerchief. These beans really do taste best served outdoors on metal or paper plates.

| | |
|---:|:---|
| 2 | cans (16 ounces each) pork and beans |
| 1 | can (16 ounces) Boston baked beans |
| 1 | can (8 ounces) crushed pineapple, drained |
| 1 | can (15 ounces) tomato sauce |
| 1 | large onion, diced |
| ¼ | pound brown sugar |
| ½ | cup dark corn syrup |
| ¼ | cup sweet pickle relish |
| ¼ | cup wine vinegar |
| 2 | tablespoons Worcestershire sauce |
| ½ to 1 | teaspoons ground pepper |
| ½ | tablespoon dry mustard |
| 4 | shakes of seasoned salt |
| 2 | shakes of hot sauce |

▪ Combine all the ingredients in a large saucepot and cook over low heat for at least 15 minutes, stirring occasionally, until the seasonings are well blended. (The mixture gains flavor as it cooks.)

*Makes 6 to 10 servings.*

---

## IF YOU COULD HAVE DINNER WITH ANYONE, WHO WOULD THAT BE?

**REGIS:** "David Letterman at Pinks Hot Dog Stand on La Brea in Los Angeles or at Gray's Papaya on 72nd and Broadway in New York City."
**KATHIE LEE:** "Barbra Streisand."

---

# PERFECT CORN ON THE COB

When corn was at its peak, Chef Tell came to the rescue with two recipes that take advantage of harvest-fresh corn. First he showed how to cook Perfect Corn on the Cob (on the stove top or on a grill), and then he demonstrated a recipe for corn fritters that uses already cooked corn.

STOVETOP VERSION

| | |
|---|---|
| 4 | *ears of corn in the husks* |
| 1 | *quart water* |
| 1 | *tablespoon salt* |
| 1 | *tablespoon granulated sugar* |
| 2 | *tablespoons butter* |

▪ Remove the husks and silk from the corn. Cut off both ends of each ear of corn.

▪ In a large saucepot, bring the water to a boil. Add the corn and the remaining ingredients and bring the water to a boil again.

▪ Turn off the heat and let the pot stand for 3 to 5 minutes. Using tongs, remove the corn from the pot and serve.

GRILLED VERSION

▪ Soak the corn in water for 30 to 60 minutes.

▪ Pull the husks back from the ears of corn, remove the silk, and then bring the husks back again over the kernels.

▪ Place the corn ears on a hot grill and cook for 5 to 8 minutes, or until heated through, turning frequently.

*Makes 2 to 4 servings.*

# CORN FRITTERS

Don't fritter away any leftover corn. Use it to make some of Chef Tell's light and airy corn fritters—a perfect accompaniment to a summertime barbecue.

3 *large eggs, separated*
1½ *cups freshly cooked corn or drained, canned corn*
½ *cup all-purpose flour*
½ *teaspoon salt*
*Pepper to taste*
*Vegetable oil, for frying*

▪ In a large bowl, beat the egg yolks until light yellow.

▪ Add the corn, flour, salt, and pepper.

▪ In another large grease-free bowl, using a hand-held electric mixer set at medium-high speed, beat the egg whites until they just start to form stiff peaks when the beaters are lifted.

▪ Using a rubber spatula, fold one-third of the beaten egg whites into the corn mixture to lighten it. Fold in the remaining egg whites.

▪ Heat the oil to 375° F. in a deep-fat fryer or a heavy saucepan.

▪ Drop the batter from a measuring tablespoon into the oil. Only cook 5 to 6 at a time, turning occasionally so that they brown evenly. Using a slotted spoon, remove the fritters to several layers of paper towels to drain. Keep warm in a 250° F. oven until ready to serve.

*Makes 4 servings.*

# CLEVER CLEAVER
# SWEET SPRING SALAD

———————

For this Clever Cleaver Brothers segment, Steve Cassarino dressed as a big bee and Lee Gerovitz dressed as a flower, and they recited the following:

Spring is upon us, it's in the air.
The Cleavers are back with a menu to share.
Great for the beach, a picnic in the park—
Try it by candlelight after dark—
Clever Spring Salad is our dish of the day,
With the bee and the flower, we'll show you the way!

| | |
|---|---|
| 1/3 | cup rice wine vinegar |
| 2 | tablespoons light-tasting olive oil |
| 2 | tablespoons honey |
| 1 | teaspoon low-sodium Angostura soy sauce |
| 1 | can (20 ounces) pineapple chunks, drained |
| 1 | can (11 ounces) mandarin orange segments, drained |
| 20 | snow peas, cut in half |
| 1 | medium cucumber, peeled and cut into chunks |
| 2/3 | cup sliced red onion |
| 1/2 | cup raisins or currants |
| 1/2 | cup shredded coconut |

▪ In a small bowl, stir together the vinegar, oil, honey, and soy sauce. Cover and refrigerate the dressing until ready to use.

▪ In a large bowl, combine the remaining ingredients. Stir the dressing and pour it over the salad. Toss to thoroughly coat the salad with the dressing. Cover and marinate for at least 1 hour to blend the flavors.

*Makes 4 servings.*

# WILD MUSHROOMS WITH GARLIC AND OLIVE OIL

During International Cooking Week on "Live" in March 1992, Marilyn Frobuccino, executive chef of the much-admired Mimosa restaurant in New York City, demonstrated this recipe, a tradition in her family that she adapted for use in the restaurant. Even Regis, who doesn't care for mushrooms, liked Marilyn's full-flavored recipe.

Marilyn recommends using a light-tasting olive oil, because a strongly flavored oil might overpower the mushrooms. Italian parsley has flat leaves and a slightly more pungent flavor than regular parsley. Marilyn also suggests accompanying this dish with crusty bread, assorted olives, and sharp provolone cheese. Serve the mushrooms in individual radicchio "cups," or surrounded by sprigs of parsley.

6   *tablespoons olive oil, divided*
3   *garlic cloves, sliced*
1   *pound assorted wild mushrooms, sliced*
    *Pinch of crushed red pepper flakes*
    *Salt and pepper to taste*
3   *ounces dry white wine or chicken broth*
2   *ounces oil-packed sun-dried tomatoes, drained and cut into strips*
3   *tablespoons chopped Italian parsley*

▪ In a large skillet, heat ¼ cup of the olive oil over medium heat. Add the garlic and cook for 2 to 3 minutes, or until lightly browned.

▪ Add the mushrooms, red pepper flakes, salt, and pepper and cook over high heat for 3 minutes, stirring occasionally. Add the wine or broth and cook until the liquid has been almost completely absorbed. Reduce the heat and add the tomatoes and parsley. Heat through and add the remaining 2 tablespoons of olive oil to "finish" the mushrooms.

*Makes 3 to 4 servings.*

*Glad* she *thinks it's funny!*

# NOODLE PUDDING

Good food goes hand in hand with delightful remembrances, and cookbook author Lora Brody combined memories with recipes most successfully in her book *Cooking with Memories*. She prepared noodle pudding, a Hanukkah favorite, for "Live" viewers. It is a versatile side dish for any time of the year. The topping makes this recipe extra-special.

NOODLE PUDDING

| | |
|---|---|
| 1 | *pound egg noodles, cooked according to package directions and drained* |
| 16 | *ounces cottage cheese* |
| 1 | *cup sour cream* |
| 8 | *ounces farmer's cheese* |
| 4 | *ounces cream cheese, at room temperature* |
| ¼ | *cup granulated sugar or firmly packed dark brown sugar* |
| 2 | *cups whole milk* |
| 6 | *large eggs, lightly beaten* |
| 6 | *tablespoons butter, melted and cooled slightly* |

TOPPING

    1    *cup apricot preserves*
    ²⁄₃   *cup sliced almonds, crushed but not finely ground*
    ¼   *cup firmly packed brown sugar*
    2    *tablespoons melted butter*

▪ Preheat the oven to 350° F. Position a rack in the center of the oven. Generously butter a 15¼-by-10¼-inch glass baking dish.

▪ Spread the cooked noodles evenly in the prepared dish.

▪ *To make the pudding:* In a large bowl, stir together the cottage cheese, sour cream, farmer's cheese, and cream cheese until blended. Stir in the sugar. Stir in the milk, eggs, and butter.

▪ Pour the mixture evenly over the noodles. Bake for 30 to 45 minutes or until the mixture is beginning to set.

▪ *Meanwhile, to make the topping:* In a small saucepan, stir together the apricot preserves, almonds, brown sugar, and butter. Cook over medium heat until the mixture is softened and well combined.

▪ Drop the mixture by spoonfuls over the noodles and spread it evenly. Return the baking dish to the oven and bake for 45 to 60 minutes longer, or until the top is browned and bubbly. Serve warm. (The cold leftovers are also delicious.)

*Makes 12 to 16 servings.*

## DO THE PHILBINS AND GIFFORDS SHARE MANY MEALS?

**KATHIE LEE:** Sure! Regis has eaten a lot of Frank's barbecued chicken and cheeseburgers. A lot of the meals we've had together have been at our house, because we have a tennis court, and Regis and Joy love tennis. So we end up eating lots of Frank's barbecue, which is just about the best in the history of the world.

# TRADITIONAL ITALIAN BREAD

Cookbook author and home economist Mary Ward appeared on "Live" to demonstrate recipes from her latest book, *The Hodgson Mill Oat Bran Cookbook*. This crusty, hearty bread is simple, yet has plenty of character, and it makes four loaves—one for now and three you can put in the freezer to enjoy later on.

Mary really made Regis participate during the segment, and he was almost up to his elbows in bread dough. His response to the "Bread Lady" was, "Why don't you just go to the store and buy a loaf of bread?" At the end of the segment, as he was buttering a slice of bread, the butter fell off and onto the floor. "Isn't that called butterfingers?" inquired Mary. "Take your last look at Bread Lady," was Regis's retort.

Mary's tip: Keep a wet towel around when you are making the bread to clean your hands and the counters. She also suggests trying the dough for making pizza crust.

|  |  |
|---|---|
|  | Non-stick cooking spray |
| 4 | cups warm (about 115° F.) water, divided |
| 1 | package (⁵⁄₁₆ ounce) active dry yeast |
| 6½ to 7 | cups Hodgson Mill 50/50 Flour |
| 1 | cup bread flour |
| 2 | teaspoons salt |

▪ Spray a large bowl with non-stick cooking spray.

▪ In a small bowl, combine 1 cup of the warm water with the yeast. Let the mixture stand for 5 minutes.

▪ In a large bowl, stir together 5 cups of the 50/50 flour with the bread flour.

▪ In another large bowl, combine the remaining 3 cups of water with the salt. Stir in the yeast mixture. Gradually pour the flour mixture into the water, stirring as you add the flour. When the dough is stiff, turn it onto a floured board and knead it for about 10 minutes, or until it forms a smooth, elastic ball. Add additional flour if necessary.

▪ Place the ball of dough in the prepared bowl and turn the dough to coat it thoroughly. Cover the bowl with plastic wrap, then with a damp towel, and let the dough rise in a warm, draft-free place for about 1 hour. It will almost double in bulk.

▪ Spray a baking sheet with non-stick cooking spray. Turn the dough onto a floured board and knead slightly. Cut the dough into 4 pieces and form these into 4 loaves, each about 12 inches long and 3 inches wide. Place the loaves on the prepared baking sheet and let rise in a warm, draft-free place for about 1 hour.

▪ Preheat the oven to 425° F.

▪ Bake the loaves for 35 to 45 minutes. (During the first few minutes of baking, place 3 to 4 ice cubes on the oven floor to create steam. This will make a crisp crust.) Remove the loaves from the sheet and reduce the oven temperature to 350° F. Put the bread back in the oven directly on the oven rack to finish baking. Bake about 20 minutes longer, or until the loaves are golden brown and sound hollow when tapped on the bottom.

*Makes 4 loaves of bread.*

*Variations*: You can also use a mixture of half whole wheat and half all-purpose flour. Try making the bread with a little rye or buckwheat flour for a slightly different flavor and texture.

# *I*RISH FRECKLE BREAD

Alan Thicke was a delightful guest on "Live." Though neither he nor Regis are skilled chefs, they were easily able to pull off making this delicious bread recipe. Alan was on the show to promote National Family Week and to encourage families to cook together. This bread has an excellent texture and a mild flavor because it uses cooked mashed potatoes. (Dates form the "freckles.")

5 to 5½    *cups all-purpose flour, divided*

½    *cup granulated sugar*

2    *packages of Fleischmann's RapidRise Yeast*

¾    *teaspoon salt*

1    *cup water (reserved from boiling the potatoes or use tap water)*

½    *cup (1 stick) butter or margarine*

2    *large eggs, at room temperature*

⅓    *cup cooked mashed potatoes (or ¼ cup instant potato flakes, stirred with ⅓ cup boiling water and allowed to cool), at room temperature*

1    *cup chopped dates*

▪ In a large bowl, combine 2 cups of the flour with the sugar, yeast, and salt. Heat the water and the butter until very warm (125° to 130° F.).

▪ Gradually stir the warm liquid into the dry ingredients. Stir in the eggs, mashed potatoes, dates, and enough of the additional flour to make a soft dough.

▪ Knead the dough on a lightly floured surface for 8 to 10 minutes, or until it is smooth and elastic. Cover the dough and let it rest for 10 minutes. (Alan said, "It's tired, it needs to rest.")

▪ Generously butter two 8½-by-4½-inch loaf pans. Divide the dough into 4 equal-sized pieces. Shape each piece into a slender loaf about 8½ inches long. Set 2 loaves in each of the prepared pans.

▪ Cover and let rise in a warm, draft-free place about 1 hour, or until doubled in bulk.

▪ Preheat the oven to 350° F.

▪ Bake for 35 to 40 minutes, or until the bread is baked through and sounds hollow when tapped on the bottom. Remove the loaves from the pans and set aside to cool completely on a wire rack.

*Makes 2 loaves of bread.*

*Rise & Shine!*

# BING CHERRY CRUMB CAKE

Carole Walter's book *Great Cakes* is filled with exactly what its title promises, and this recipe is a shining example. Try Carole's delicious recipe for brunch or as a delightful dessert for a summer meal, served with vanilla ice cream, sweetened whipped cream, or lightly sweetened yogurt.

### CRUMB MIXTURE

| | |
|---|---|
| 1/2 | cup unsifted unbleached all-purpose flour |
| 1/2 | cup pecans |
| 2 | tablespoons firmly packed light brown sugar |
| 1/8 | teaspoon baking powder |
| 3 | tablespoons unsalted butter, melted and cooled |

### CAKE MIXTURE

| | |
|---|---|
| 1 | cup sifted unbleached all-purpose flour |
| 1 | teaspoon baking powder |
| 1/4 | teaspoon salt |
| 1/2 | cup (1 stick) unsalted butter |
| 2/3 | cup granulated sugar |
| 3 | large eggs |
| 1/2 | teaspoon vanilla extract |
| 1 | pound Bing cherries, pitted |

▪ Generously butter a 9-inch springform pan. Line the pan with baking parchment and then generously butter the paper.

▪ *To make the crumb mixture:* Place the flour, pecans, brown sugar, and baking powder in the container of a food processor fitted with the metal blade. Pulse 6 or 8 times, or until the nuts are finely chopped. Add the butter. Pulse 2 to 3 times, or until the mixture forms pea-size crumbs. Do not overprocess.

▪ Sprinkle one-third of the crumbs evenly over the bottom of the pre-pared pan. Reserve the remaining two-thirds for the topping. Press the crumbs down lightly in the pan to form a bottom crust. Set aside.

▪ Position a rack in the lower third of the oven and preheat to 350° F.

▪ *To make the cake:* Using a triple sifter, sift together the flour, baking powder, and salt and reserve.

▪ Cut the butter into 1-inch pieces and place them in the large bowl of an electric mixer fitted with beaters or the paddle attachment. Mix on low speed to soften. Increase the speed to medium-high and cream for about 1½ to 2 minutes, or until the mixture is smooth and light.

▪ One tablespoon at a time, add the sugar, taking 3 to 4 minutes to blend it well. Scrape down the sides of the bowl occasionally.

▪ One at a time at 1-minute intervals, add the eggs, scraping the sides of the bowl as necessary. Blend in the vanilla.

▪ Reduce the mixer speed to low. In three additions, add the flour mix-ture, beating just until incorporated after each addition. Mix for about 15 seconds longer.

▪ Carefully spread the batter over the crumb layer in the pan and arrange the cherries in rings on top. Use about 20 cherries to form the outer cir-cle, working inward to 15, 10, and 3 in the center. Sprinkle the reserved crumbs on top of the cherries.

▪ Center the pan on the oven rack and bake in the preheated oven for 60 to 65 minutes, or until the cake begins to come away from the side of the pan and the top is golden brown. Remove the pan from the oven and set on a wire rack to cool.

▪ Cover the pan with a piece of aluminum foil, pressing it snugly against the sides to hold in the topping. Invert the cake onto the rack. Lift off the pan and carefully peel off the parchment. Turn the cake right side up onto a serving plate. To store the cake, cover it loosely with aluminum foil and store at room temperature for 1 to 2 days or, refrigerated, for up to 5 days. Reheat in a 350° F. oven for about 5 minutes and serve slightly warm.

*Makes 8 to 10 servings.*

## WHAT WAS YOUR FAVORITE FOOD GROWING UP?

**KATHIE LEE:** I have great memories of food, because my mom was a fabulous cook. As a special morning treat, she would make us fried bread. I can't imagine anything more artery-clogging or high-fat, but boy, was it delicious!

# HONEY-NUT APPLE MUFFINS

Fred Griffith is the cohost of Cleveland's "The Morning Exchange." He and his wife, Linda, a cooking teacher and journalist, appeared on "Live" while promoting their cookbook, *The Best of the Midwest*. After eating 130 meals out in 11 months, the Griffiths selected 32 restaurants to feature in their book. This recipe is from the River Wildlife Restaurant, a part of the American Club, in Kohler, Wisconsin.

A tip: Measure the oil first, so that the honey will easily slide right out of the oiled measuring cup.

| | |
|---|---|
| 4¼ | cups all-purpose flour, divided |
| 1 | cup firmly packed dark brown sugar |
| ½ | cup granulated sugar |
| 5 | tablespoons butter, melted |
| 2 | tablespoons baking powder |
| 1 | teaspoon salt |
| 2 | cups milk |
| ¾ | cup honey |
| ½ | cup vegetable oil |
| 2 | large eggs |
| 2 | cups chopped apples, peeled or unpeeled |
| ½ | cup chopped walnuts or hazelnuts |

■ Position one oven rack in the top third of the oven and one rack in the bottom third of the oven. Preheat the oven to 375° F. Generously butter twenty-four 3-by-1¼-inch (3½- to 4-ounce) muffin cups.

■ In a small bowl, stir together ¼ cup of the flour, the sugars, and the butter until combined. Reserve this topping.

■ In a large bowl, stir together the remaining 4 cups of flour, baking powder, and salt. In another bowl, stir together the milk, honey, oil, and eggs. Stir in the apples and nuts. Make a well in the center of the dry ingredients; add the milk mixture, and stir just to combine. Do not overmix.

■ Spoon the batter evenly into the prepared muffin cups and sprinkle an equal amount of the reserved topping over each muffin. Bake for 15 to 20 minutes, or until a cake tester inserted in the center of one muffin comes out clean.

■ Remove the muffin cups to a wire rack. Let cool for 5 minutes before removing the muffins from the cups; finish cooling the muffins on the rack. Serve the muffins warm, or cool them completely and store in an airtight container in the refrigerator.

*Makes 24 muffins.*

Steve Friedman/Buena Vista Television

*Regis is almost jumping out of his seat. Is all that energy coming straight from the coffee?*

# BLUEBERRY OAT MUFFINS

When Phyllis Kaufman, author of *The Good Eating, Good Health Cookbook*, appeared on the show, the studio was filled with the luscious smell of fresh blueberry muffins. Phyllis's recipe makes several healthful changes in standard muffin recipes—she has eliminated egg yolks and used only the whites, replaced whole milk with skim milk, and substituted poly-unsaturated margarine for butter. But she does add a spicy brown sugar topping as a sweet finish to these breakfast gems. One (or more) would be a welcome addition to a lunchbag.

## MUFFINS

| | |
|---|---|
| ³/₄ | cup oat flour |
| ¹/₂ | cup oat bran |
| ¹/₂ | cup all-purpose flour |
| 1 | tablespoon baking powder |
| 1 | teaspoon ground cinnamon |
| ¹/₂ | cup firmly packed dark brown sugar |
| ¹/₄ | cup (¹/₂ stick) polyunsaturated margarine, at room temperature |
| 3 | large egg whites |
| ³/₄ | cup skim milk |
| 2 | cups fresh or frozen blueberries |

## TOPPING

| | |
|---|---|
| 3 | tablespoons all-purpose flour |
| 1 | tablespoon polyunsaturated margarine |
| 2 | teaspoons granulated sugar |
| 2 | teaspoons firmly packed dark brown sugar |
| ¹/₂ | teaspoon ground cinnamon |

▪ Preheat the oven to 400° F. Generously butter twelve 3-by-1¼-inch (3½- to 4-ounce) muffin cups.

▪ In a large bowl, stir together the oat flour, oat bran, all-purpose flour, baking powder, and cinnamon until combined.

▪ In another bowl, cream together the brown sugar and margarine until combined. Stir in the egg whites. Stir in the milk.

▪ Add the brown sugar mixture and the blueberries to the dry ingredients. Mix lightly, taking care not to overmix.

▪ In a medium bowl, stir together the topping ingredients until combined.

▪ Spoon the batter evenly into the prepared muffin cups; sprinkle an even amount of the reserved topping over each muffin. Bake for 15 minutes if you used fresh blueberries, or 25 minutes if you used frozen blueberries, or until the muffins are golden brown.

▪ Remove the muffin cups to a wire rack. Let cool for 5 minutes before removing the muffins from the cups; finish cooling the muffins on the rack. You can serve the muffins warm or cool them completely.

*Makes 12 muffins.*

## BLUEBERRIES—ALL-AMERICAN FRUIT

Wild blueberries were growing in North America long before the first colonists arrived, and these days 95 percent of the world's commercially harvested blueberries are grown on this continent. When blueberries appear in quantity in the markets, it is one of the signs that summer has arrived. While the blueberry season stretches from early May to September, the berries are at their peak from mid-June to mid-August.

Fresh blueberries should be covered and refrigerated. They will keep for up to three weeks. If you plan to freeze fresh blueberries, place the berries in a single layer on a jelly-roll pan. Freeze the berries and then transfer them to freezer containers. Properly frozen, berries will keep for up to two years. Both fresh and frozen berries should be rinsed and drained just before serving. Frozen blueberries should not be thawed and refrozen as this will affect their quality.

In addition to tasting delicious, blueberries are a good source of fiber, potassium, and Vitamin C.

*There are broad smiles aplenty on the Mother's Day celebration show.*

# MOTHER'S DAY TURNOVER

Make this recipe as a special treat for your mom on Mother's Day. The Love Chef creates everything with love and this is yet another of his easy and delicious recipes—and a great way to jazz up pancakes. Add sliced fresh fruit as a colorful topping.

| | |
|---|---|
| 8 | ounces ricotta cheese or cottage cheese |
| 1/3 | cup confectioners' sugar, plus extra for sprinkling |
| 1/2 | teaspoon vanilla extract |
| | Fresh fruit preserves, warmed |
| 8 | 6-inch thin pancakes, freshly cooked |

▪ In a medium bowl, stir together the ricotta cheese, 1/3 cup of the confectioners' sugar, and vanilla extract.

▪ Spread the preserves across the middle of each just-cooked pancake. Top with the ricotta mixture and roll each pancake over to enclose the mixture. Sprinkle with confectioners' sugar and "serve with love."

*Makes 4 servings.*

# EASY FRENCH CRÊPES

Martin Woesle, chef of the esteemed restaurant Mille Fleurs in Rancho Santa Fe, was invited to be a guest on the show at Regis's recommendation. Martin uses these versatile crêpes as a basis for many different dessert and brunch combinations. He suggests adding some chopped pistachios to the batter before making the crêpes. Fill the crêpes, as Martin does, with sliced fresh peaches and serve with a caramel sauce. Or you can toss blood oranges with orange liqueur and use them as a crêpe filling. The tartness of the oranges would be perfectly balanced with a creamy white chocolate sauce.

| | |
|---|---|
| 1/2 | cup sifted all-purpose flour |
| 2 | large eggs |
| 2 | tablespoons granulated sugar |
| 1 | tablespoon unsalted butter, melted, plus 1 teaspoon, for greasing the skillet |
| | Pinch of salt |
| 3/4 | cup milk, heated |

■ In a large bowl, whisk together the flour, eggs, sugar, the 1 tablespoon of melted butter, and the salt until smooth. Whisk in the milk and mix again until smooth.

■ In an 8-inch non-stick skillet over medium-high heat, melt the 1 teaspoon of butter.

■ Add 3 tablespoons of the batter to the pan and tip the pan so that the bottom is evenly coated. Cook for 10 to 15 seconds, or until the crêpe begins to brown, then turn it over with a heatproof rubber spatula. Cook the second side for 5 to 10 seconds. Flip the crêpe out of the pan onto an inverted plate to cool. Repeat the process until the batter is used up. Keep the crêpes warm in a warm oven.

■ To store any unused crêpes, let the crêpes cool completely, then stack them between sheets of waxed paper, cover, and refrigerate.

*Makes about 10 crêpes.*

# SWEETHEART FRITTATA

Not surprisingly, this lovely recipe comes from the Love Chef, Francis Anthony. Breakfast is one of the best times to be nice to the one you love, and this recipe is just right for that special someone (plus leftovers for any others you care about!). It's a marvelous way to use up any cooked potatoes you may have saved from dinner the night before.

| | |
|---|---|
| 3 | medium red potatoes, thoroughly scrubbed |
| 3 | tablespoons olive oil |
| 3 | tablespoons unsalted butter |
| 1 | red pepper, seeded and thinly sliced |
| 1 | medium onion, thinly sliced |
| 8 | large eggs |
| 1 | cup shredded Jarlsberg cheese |
| ½ | teaspoon dried thyme leaves |
| | Freshly ground pepper to taste |

▪ Cook the potatoes in boiling salted water for about 20 minutes, or until they are tender when pierced with the point of a sharp knife. Drain the potatoes and cut into ½-inch-thick slices.

▪ In a large (10-inch) skillet, heat the oil and butter over medium-high heat. Add the potatoes, red pepper, and onion, and cook, stirring from time to time, for 5 to 7 minutes, or until the onions are translucent.

▪ In a medium bowl, beat the eggs until frothy. Stir in the cheese, thyme, and pepper. Pour the mixture evenly into the skillet and shake it into place over the vegetables. Continue cooking for about 4 to 6 minutes. As the egg mixture starts to set, lift the edges and let the liquid mixture run underneath.

▪ When the bottom is formed and browned, place a large plate over the skillet, flip, and then slide the frittata back into the pan to cook the top. If you do not feel confident enough to do this, place the skillet under the broiler for 3 to 4 minutes. (Make sure to wrap the handle with aluminum foil if it is not ovenproof.)

*Makes 4 to 6 servings.*

# QUICHE

Regis said that he thought that Chef Tell's quiche is the best he has ever tasted and that real men *do* eat quiche. And, of course, he's right!

| | |
|---|---|
| 1 | (9-inch) unbaked pie crust |
| ²/₃ | cup diced boiled ham |
| ³/₄ | cup shredded Swiss cheese |
| 4 | large eggs |
| 1 | cup heavy cream |
| 2 | tablespoons finely chopped fresh parsley |
| | Dash of freshly grated nutmeg |
| | Salt and pepper to taste |

▪ Preheat the oven to 400° F.

▪ With the tines of a fork, pierce the pie crust in several places.

▪ Sprinkle the ham evenly over the bottom of the pie crust. Then sprinkle the cheese over the ham.

▪ In a large bowl, whisk the eggs and cream together until well blended. Stir in the parsley, nutmeg, salt, and pepper. Pour the mixture into the pie crust. Bake about 25 minutes, or until the filling is set and golden.

*Makes 6 to 8 servings.*

---

## WHAT ARE YOUR LEAST-FAVORITE FOODS?

**REGIS:** "Escargots (snails), lima beans, brussels sprouts, sweetbreads, or foods that are too spicy."
**KATHIE LEE:** "Green peppers and squash."

# COCOA WAFFLES

Barbara Albright, the editor of this book and former editor-in-chief of *Chocolatier*, created these cocoa waffles originally for a special Valentine's Day issue of the magazine. If you want to celebrate the day, too, use a heart-shaped waffle iron, dust with powdered sugar, and serve with fresh red raspberries for an elegant breakfast in bed. These chocolaty waffles can also be used as a dessert: Top each one with a scoop of your favorite ice cream, then drizzle with chocolate sauce and add whipped cream and a sprinkling of chopped walnuts for a totally decadent finishing touch.

| | |
|---|---|
| 1²/₃ | *cups cake flour* |
| ¹/₃ | *cup unsweetened non-alkalized cocoa powder (such as Hershey's)* |
| ¹/₃ | *cup granulated sugar* |
| 1¹/₂ | *teaspoons baking powder* |
| 1 | *teaspoon baking soda* |
| ¹/₂ | *teaspoon salt* |
| 1¹/₂ | *cups buttermilk* |
| ¹/₂ | *cup (1 stick) unsalted butter, melted* |
| 2 | *large eggs, separated* |
| 2 | *teaspoons vanilla extract* |

▪ Preheat the waffle iron according to the manufacturer's instructions. (The iron is ready when a few drops of water sprinkled onto the surface immediately turn into dancing droplets.)

▪ In a large bowl, stir together the flour, cocoa, sugar, baking powder, baking soda, and salt. In another bowl, stir together the buttermilk, butter, egg yolks, and vanilla. Make a well in the center of the flour mixture. Add the liquid ingredients and stir just to combine.

▪ In a grease-free medium bowl, using a hand-held electric mixer set at medium-high speed, beat the egg whites until they just start to form stiff peaks when the beaters are lifted.

▪ Using a rubber spatula, fold one-third of the beaten egg whites into the batter to lighten it. Fold in the remaining egg whites.

▪ Pour the mixture into the center of the preheated waffle iron, filling it about two-thirds full (a heaping ⅓ cup per waffle). Cook the waffles for 3 to 5 minutes, or until they are set (steam will stop coming out from the edges). Transfer the waffles to a warm oven and continue making waffles until all the batter is used.

*Makes 7 heart-shaped waffles.*

# *On the Lighter Side*

# SPICED APPLE NAPOLEON

Widely regarded as one of Boston's premier talents, Anthony Ambrose, executive chef of the Bostonian Hotel's restaurant, Seasons, prepared this delightful recipe on the show. Anthony likes to feature low-calorie, somewhat theatrical cuisine with strong, satisfying flavors.

| | |
|---|---|
| 1 | cup plus 2 tablespoons apple cider |
| 1/4 | cup firmly packed brown sugar |
| | Pinch of grated nutmeg |
| | Pinch of ground cardamom or cinnamon |
| 1 1/2 | cups diced peeled apples |
| 1/4 | cup cranberries |
| 1/2 | large apple, cored and cut into 1/8-inch-thick slices |
| | Mint leaves, for garnish (optional) |

▪ In a large skillet, bring the cider, sugar, nutmeg, and cardamom to a boil over medium heat. Add the diced apples and cranberries. Arrange the apple slices on top of the mixture in the skillet. Cover and cook for 10 to 12 minutes longer, or until the sliced apples are just tender.

▪ Using a slotted spoon, carefully transfer the sliced apples to 4 individual dessert plates, arranging them in a pinwheel design on each plate.

▪ Drain the diced apple mixture, reserving the syrup. If necessary, continue cooking the syrup for a few more minutes to thicken it.

▪ Place a mound of the diced apple mixture on top of the apple slices, drizzle with the syrup, and garnish each serving with mint leaves, if desired.

*Makes 4 servings.*

# SAFFRON APPLES WITH FROZEN PISTACHIO YOGURT

Bruce Auden of Restaurant BIGA in San Antonio, Texas, appeared on "Live" and demonstrated this recipe, which is typical of his innovative style of cooking. BIGA was selected by *Esquire* magazine as one of the 25 best new restaurants of 1991. Bruce developed this recipe especially for the show, but since that time, he reports, it has become a best-seller in his restaurant.

Saffron adds a complex flavor to this dessert. While saffron is often used by restaurant chefs, Bruce feels that home cooks are sometimes intimidated by this seasoning. Just follow his easy recipe to overcome any saffron phobia you might have.

Prepare the frozen yogurt first, but do make sure that you follow the manufacturer's instructions for your ice cream maker. (The hotel was supposed to put Bruce's ice cream maker bowl in the freezer overnight, but instead it was put in the refrigerator and his frozen yogurt for the show never froze!)

### FROZEN PISTACHIO YOGURT

| | |
|---|---|
| 2½ | teaspoons (1 envelope) unflavored gelatin |
| ¼ | cup water |
| 4 | cups plain low-fat yogurt, at room temperature |
| ⅓ | cup granulated sugar |
| 2 | teaspoons vanilla extract (preferably clear) |
| ½ | teaspoon pistachio or almond extract |
| ¼ | cup unsalted chopped pistachios, toasted |

### SAFFRON APPLES

| | |
|---|---|
| 1 | cup chenin blanc wine (Fall Creek Vineyards is ideal) |
| ¼ | gram saffron |
| 2 | tart apples, each peeled, cored, and cut into 12 wedges |
| ½ | cup apple juice |
| ½ | cup honey or barley malt |
| | Shredded coconut, for garnish (optional) |
| | Crisp dried apple rings, for garnish (optional) |

▪ *To make the yogurt:* In a small saucepan, sprinkle the gelatin over the water and let stand for 5 minutes. Place the pan over low heat and cook, stirring, for 1 to 2 minutes, or until the gelatin is dissolved.

▪ In a large bowl, stir the yogurt until it is smooth. While continuing to stir, add the gelatin mixture, sugar, and vanilla and pistachio extracts. Stir until blended.

▪ Transfer the mixture to an ice cream maker and freeze according to the manufacturer's instructions. When nearly frozen, stir in the pistachios and continue to freeze completely. This yogurt is best served straight from the ice cream maker, but it may be kept frozen for up to 7 days.

*Makes 6 ½-cup servings.*

▪ *To make the Saffron Apples:* Combine the wine and saffron in a small bowl and let stand for at least 1 hour or for up to 4 hours.

▪ In a small heavy saucepan, combine the apples, saffron wine, apple juice, and honey. (Select a saucepan small enough that the apples are covered with the liquid.) Over medium heat, bring the mixture to a simmer for 5 to 7 minutes, or until the apple wedges are tender, but still firm.

▪ Using a slotted spoon, carefully transfer the cooked apples to a bowl and refrigerate to cool. Meanwhile, continue to boil the liquid in the saucepan until it is reduced to ¾ cup. Pour this reduced liquid over the apples and cool for at least 1 hour.

▪ To serve, arrange 4 servings of apples on white plates and add about 1 ounce of the liquid to each one. Top each plate with a scoop of the Frozen Pistachio Yogurt and garnish with shredded coconut and crisp dried apple rings, if desired.

*Makes 4 servings.*

## WHAT MEALS HAVE YOU HAD WITH FAMOUS PEOPLE?

**KATHIE LEE:** I once had dinner with Mikhail Baryshnikov. We ate at Jack's, a restaurant on the East Side in New York City. I also ate at the White House, at a state dinner for the President of South Korea. My dinner partner was Secretary of State James A. Baker. Anytime I am sitting next to a person of that stature, food becomes secondary to me, so I don't remember what I ate!

# PERSIMMON AND MAPLE FOOL

Peter George of Peter's Restaurant in Indianapolis, Indiana, was one of the winners of "Live"'s Diet Dessert Challenge. Peter prefers the recipe made with fresh persimmons (which are available at most supermarkets in the winter months), but persimmon pulp can be found in the freezer sections of specialty stores or mail-ordered (see page 246). When he was asked for a more everyday substitute, he suggested sweet potatoes. At his restaurant, Peter changes the menu on a monthly basis to take advantage of the freshest seasonal Midwestern produce. Since his appearance on "Live," he says, business has boomed!

| | |
|---|---|
| 1 | cup persimmon pulp, divided |
| 1½ | tablespoons water |
| 2½ | teaspoons (1 envelope) unflavored gelatin |
| 1½ | cups plain low-fat yogurt |
| ½ | cup heavy cream |
| ¼ | cup maple syrup |
| 1 | tablespoon light molasses |
| ½ | teaspoon ground cinnamon |
| ¼ | teaspoon ground allspice |
| | Apple wedges, pear wedges, and additional maple syrup, for garnish (optional) |

▪ In a heatproof bowl, combine ¼ cup of the persimmon pulp, the water, and gelatin. Let stand for 5 minutes.

▪ Set the bowl over a pan of simmering water and stir until the gelatin is dissolved. Remove the bowl from the heat and stir in the remaining ¾ cup of persimmon pulp.

▪ In a chilled bowl, using an electric mixer, whip the yogurt. In another chilled bowl, whip the cream until soft peaks form. Fold the whipped cream, maple syrup, molasses, cinnamon, and allspice into the yogurt, then fold in the persimmon mixture.

▪ Chill the mixture for 3 to 4 hours, or until set. Scoop portions of the persimmon mixture onto 4 dessert plates. Garnish each serving with apple and pear wedges and drizzle with additional maple syrup, if desired.

*Makes 4 servings.*

# Shrimp and Vegetables

At Benihana restaurants, each table has a hibachi grill and its own personal chef, who cooks the meal using what the chain's founder, Rocky Aoki, calls "the art of Japanese cooking, where the hibachi table is the chef's canvas." Rocky and one of his master chefs prepared this simple dish, which is low in both fat and calories, to celebrate Benihana's 25th anniversary. The evening he appeared on the show, many of his restaurants were honoring the day by featuring celebrity chefs and donating the proceeds to help fight juvenile diabetes.

| | |
|---|---|
| 3 | pounds shrimp |
| | Salt to taste |
| 4 | teaspoons soybean oil |
| 2 | zucchini, sliced |
| 8 | large mushrooms, sliced |
| 1 | onion, sliced |
| ¼ | cup freshly squeezed lemon juice |

▪ Peel and devein the shrimp. To devein the shrimp, using the point of a sharp knife, make a shallow cut down the center back (the curved side) of each shrimp and remove the dark vein. Rinse away any bits of the vein that remain. Season with salt.

▪ In a wok or a large skillet, heat the oil over medium-high heat. Add the shrimp and cook for about 3 minutes on each side, or until cooked through. Transfer to a hot platter and keep warm.

▪ Add the zucchini, mushrooms, and onion to the hot skillet and cook for 3 to 5 minutes, or until they are just crisp-tender. Add the vegetables to the platter with the shrimp and sprinkle with the lemon juice.

*Makes 8 servings.*

# *T*UCSON *C*HICKEN

This is another recipe from Janos Wilder, who was on the show to promote his cookbook, *Recipes and Tales from a Southwest Restaurant*, based on his experiences at his namesake restaurant in Tucson, Arizona. Though it is inspired by classic French techniques, this one-skillet dish is delightfully straightforward to make.

| | |
|---|---|
| 2 | *tablespoons olive oil, divided* |
| 1 | *onion, cut into julienne strips* |
| 1 | *red bell pepper, seeded and cut into julienne strips* |
| ½ | *pound small mushrooms, cut in half* |
| 1 | *cup red wine, divided* |
| ¼ | *cup chopped garlic* |
| ¼ | *cup tomato paste* |
| | *All-purpose flour for dredging the chicken* |
| | *Salt and pepper to taste* |
| 1 | *2½-pound chicken cut into pieces* |
| 2 | *cups chopped fresh basil leaves* |
| 4 | *cups chicken broth* |
| 3 | *plum tomatoes, diced* |
| | *Freshly cooked noodles* |

▪ In a large skillet, heat 1 tablespoon of the oil over medium-high heat. Add the onion and red pepper and cook for 3 to 4 minutes until softened slightly, stirring frequently.

▪ Add the mushrooms, ½ cup of the wine, the garlic, and the tomato paste and cook 5 minutes longer.

▪ Season about 1½ cups of all-purpose flour with salt and pepper. Dip the chicken in the seasoned flour to lightly coat both sides; shake off any excess.

■ In a Dutch oven or a large heavy saucepot, heat the remaining 1 table-spoon of oil. Cook the chicken for 5 to 7 minutes on each side, or until lightly browned.

■ Add the cooked vegetables to the saucepot of chicken. Then stir in the basil and add the chicken broth and the remaining ½ cup of red wine. Cover the pot and simmer for 30 minutes, stirring occasionally. Add the tomatoes, cover, and simmer for 15 minutes longer. Serve over noodles.

*Makes 4 to 6 servings.*

# TEXAS-STYLE CHICKEN OR BEEF SKILLET

Cookbook author Mary Ward from Cleveland, Ohio, first started cooking with oat bran to help lower her husband's cholesterol. After sampling this recipe, Regis proclaimed, "I can't taste the oat bran!" Mary actually served the dish with oat bran tortillas to boost the fiber content even higher. Try making this as a change of pace from oat bran muffins.

| | |
|---|---|
| 1 | *pound boneless, skinless chicken breast or lean round steak* |
| 1 | *tablespoon peanut oil* |
| 1 | *can (22 ounces) chili hot beans* |
| 2 | *large tomatoes, chopped* |
| 1 | *cup uncooked oat bran hot cereal* |
| ¾ | *cup finely chopped onion* |
| 3 | *tablespoons finely chopped green bell pepper* |
| 1½ | *teaspoons chili powder* |
| ½ | *teaspoon garlic powder* |
| ½ | *cup water* |
| ¾ | *cup shredded Monterey jack cheese with jalapeños* |
| 16 | *oat bran or corn tortillas, warmed* |

■ Cut the chicken or beef slices into ½-inch-wide strips.

■ In a large skillet, heat the oil over medium-high heat until hot. Quickly cook the chicken or beef for 2 to 3 minutes, or until the strips are no longer pink. Add the undrained beans, tomatoes, oat bran, onion, green pepper, chili powder, garlic powder, and water. Simmer for about 20 minutes, or until the vegetables are tender, stirring occasionally.

■ Top the skillet evenly with the shredded cheese. Cover for about 2 minutes, or until the layer of cheese has melted. Serve with tortillas.

*Makes 8 servings.*

# $J$O JO'S JUICY SHRIMP

Jean-Georges Vongerichten started cooking in Europe at the age of 15. Not too long ago, he was drinking a glass of carrot juice every morning, and the inspiration came to him to use juices as a way to add flavor to foods without adding excess fat. That seemingly simple concept led him to create a whole new style of cooking that has delighted discerning New York diners at his Upper East Side restaurant, Jo Jo. Jean-George says he selected this recipe to demonstrate on "Live" because "it is very simple and healthy. I like the combination of the sea meeting the ground."

|  |  |
|---|---|
| 2 | *pounds shrimp* |
| 10 | *medium carrots, juiced, or 2 cups carrot juice* |
|  | *Pinch of ground cinnamon* |
|  | *Pinch of ground cloves* |
| 1 | *teaspoon freshly squeezed lemon juice* |
| 6 | *tablespoons unsalted butter, divided* |
|  | *Salt and cayenne pepper to taste* |
| 2 | *tablespoons chopped fresh chervil* |

Steve Friedman/Buena Vista Television

*Regis gives Jean-Georges Vongerichten a few culinary pointers of his own.*

▪ Peel and devein the shrimp. To devein the shrimp, using the point of a sharp knife, make a shallow cut down the center back (the curved side) of each shrimp and remove the dark vein. Rinse away any bits of the vein that remain.

▪ In a saucepan, combine the carrot juice, cinnamon, cloves, and lemon juice. Heat until warm over medium-high heat. Cut 4 individual tablespoons of the butter. One at a time, whisk each one until combined. Continue to cook until the mixture comes to a boil, stirring occasionally. Remove the pan from the heat and keep warm.

▪ In a large skillet, heat the remaining 2 tablespoons of butter over medium-high heat until melted. Add the shrimp and cook for about 1½ minutes on each side, or until the shrimp are pink. Season with salt and cayenne.

▪ Serve the shrimp with the sauce and sprinkle with the chervil.

*Makes 6 servings.*

# Potato Latkes

———————— ▪□▪ ————————

Latkes are usually higher in fat and sodium than the following flavorful version from Francine Prince. In Jewish households latkes are traditionally served at Hanukkah but they are also nice as a change from rice and standard potato side dishes—and they would be great for brunch! No matter when you serve them, Francine suggests accompanying them with applesauce or sour cream.

| | |
|---:|:---|
| 4 | medium potatoes (1¾ pounds), preferably Idaho potatoes, peeled and finely grated |
| 1 | tablespoon freshly squeezed lemon juice |
| 1 | large egg yolk |
| 2 | large egg whites |
| ½ | teaspoon freshly grated nutmeg |
| ½ | teaspoon ground ginger |
| ½ | teaspoon granulated sugar |
| ¼ | teaspoon salt |
| ¼ | teaspoon coarsely ground black pepper |
| 5 to 6 | tablespoons matzoh meal |
| ⅓ | cup finely chopped onion |
| 1½ | tablespoons finely chopped garlic |
| 1½ | tablespoons chopped fresh dill or parsley |
| | Non-stick cooking spray |
| About 2½ | tablespoons Italian olive oil |

▪ Squeeze the potatoes to remove as much moisture as possible and then place them in a large bowl. Add the lemon juice and toss to combine.

▪ In a small bowl, beat the egg yolk and whites with the nutmeg, ginger, sugar, salt, and pepper. Add the egg mixture to the potato mixture and stir to combine. Fold in 5 tablespoons of the matzoh meal and the onion, garlic, and dill. Let stand for 5 minutes. Add the remaining 1 tablespoon of matzoh meal, if necessary, to make a batter that is fairly thick and holds together.

Steve Friedman/Buena Vista Television

*Sitting pretty!*

▪ Spray 1 or 2 large non-stick skillets with non-stick cooking spray. Heat about 1 tablespoon of the olive oil in each skillet over medium-high heat. Start making the pancakes when a few drops of water sprinkled onto the surface immediately turn into dancing droplets.

▪ Drop 4 to 5 heaping tablespoons of the potato mixture into each skillet. Flatten each mound into a pancake about 3 inches in diameter.

▪ Cook each pancake for about 3 minutes on each side, or until golden brown, adjusting the heat, if necessary, to prevent burning. Drain the pancakes on paper towels. Keep the pancakes in a warm oven while you continue to make the rest. Repeat until all the pancake mixture has been used, adding more oil as necessary. Serve immediately.

*Makes about 20 3-inch pancakes.*

*Variation*: For puffy pancakes, add the 1 egg yolk in the first part of the recipe. Beat the 2 egg whites until stiff peaks form and fold the egg-white mixture into the batter after all the ingredients have been added.

---

## HOW DO YOU MAINTAIN YOUR TRIM FIGURES?

**REGIS:** "My personal trainer at Radu's, Boris (which means 'pain' in Russian). I try to work out four times a week. I also watch my cholesterol."

**KATHIE LEE:** "A SlimFast bar for breakfast, anything for lunch, running on a treadmill, a light dinner, and chasing a toddler!"

---

# CHOCOLATE LOVE BITES

Love Chef Francis Anthony developed these confections with both taste and good health in mind.

| | |
|---|---|
| ¼ | cup safflower oil |
| ½ | cup unsweetened cocoa powder |
| 2¼ | cups confectioners' sugar |
| ¼ | cup evaporated skim milk |
| 1 | teaspoon vanilla extract |
| ½ | cup raisins, chopped nuts, or chopped candied mixed fruits |
| | Confectioners' sugar or unsweetened cocoa powder |

▪ In a medium bowl, whisk together the oil and cocoa powder until combined.

▪ Stir in the 2 cups of confectioners' sugar.

▪ Using an electric mixer, beat in the evaporated milk and vanilla at low speed until smooth. Stir in the raisins, chopped nuts, or candied fruits. Cover the bowl and refrigerate overnight, or until firm.

▪ Shape the mixture into 1-inch balls. Roll in confectioners' sugar or cocoa powder. Store in the refrigerator in a covered container between sheets of waxed paper until ready to serve.

*Makes 20 confections.*

# LOW-CAL CHOCOLATE BROWNIES

Susan S. Schiffman, Ph.D., is a professor of medical psychology at Duke Medical Center and director of Duke's weight-loss unit. A specialist in flavor and texture, she developed the Nutri/System Flavor Set Point Theory. This states that people who are overweight crave greatly intensified flavors and varied textures in their foods. When overweight people are offered foods with a range of flavors and textures, they normally eat smaller quantities and are better able to control their appetites. Susan designed these brownies with this concept in mind, so they are packed with chocolate flavor and have a chewy texture. On "Live" the brownies were taste-tested against several other kinds, and Joy and Regis liked them the best. Bake up a batch and we'll let you be the judge!

|        | *Non-stick cooking spray* |
|--------|--------------------------|
| 2½     | *tablespoons margarine, softened* |
| ⅓      | *cup granulated sugar* |
| ¼      | *cup unsweetened cocoa powder* |
| 1      | *large egg* |
| ½      | *cup, less 1 tablespoon, sifted all-purpose unbleached flour* |
| 1½     | *tablespoons chopped walnuts* |

▪ Preheat the oven to 350° F. Lightly spray a 7½-by-3½-inch loaf pan with non-stick cooking spray.

▪ In a 1-quart bowl, using an electric mixer, cream together the margarine and sugar. Stir in the cocoa powder, then add the egg, and blend on low for 30 seconds, scraping down the sides of the bowl. Continue beating for 30 seconds longer.

▪ Sift in the flour and stir until well incorporated. Stir in the nuts. Scrape the batter into the prepared pan and spread it evenly. Bake for 18 minutes, or until a cake tester inserted into the center comes out slightly moist. Transfer the pan to a wire rack to cool completely. When cool, cut into 10 squares.

*Makes 10 brownies.*

*Grand*
*Finales*

# CHOCOLATE PECAN PIE

Craig Claiborne is one of the leading culinary experts in the United States and a long-time writer and editor for *The New York Times*. He appeared on "Live" to promote *The Revised New York Times Cookbook*. The original has long been a definitive guide for cooks at all levels.

With the addition of pure chocolate, in the form of unsweetened chocolate squares, Craig brings pecan pie to a new level of decadence. If you don't have pecans, try substituting other nuts in this easy recipe.

| | |
|---|---|
| 3 | ounces unsweetened chocolate |
| 2 | tablespoons butter |
| 1 | cup light corn syrup |
| ¾ | cup granulated sugar |
| 1 | teaspoon vanilla extract |
| 3 | large eggs, lightly beaten |
| 1 | cup chopped pecans |
| 1 | unbaked (9-inch) pie shell |
| ½ | cup heavy cream |

▪ Preheat the oven to 375° F.

▪ In the top of a double boiler over hot, not simmering, water, heat the chocolate and butter until melted and smooth.

▪ In a heavy saucepan, combine the corn syrup and sugar and bring to a boil over high heat. Boil 2 minutes.

▪ Stir together the chocolate mixture, syrup mixture, and vanilla. Very gradually, whisk the chocolate mixture into the eggs, whisking constantly until all the chocolate is added and the mixture is well blended. Stir in the pecans.

▪ Scrape the mixture into the pie shell. Bake for 40 to 50 minutes, or until the pie is puffed across the top. Transfer the pie to a wire rack to cool.

▪ In a cold bowl, using an electric mixer with cold beaters, beat the cream just until peaks begin to form. Cut the pie into wedges and serve with the whipped cream.

*Makes 8 to 12 servings.*

# Chocolate Whipped Cream Pie

Russell Dingeldein, pastry chef of the Hotel Hershey in Hershey, Pennsylvania—a town forever identified with chocolate—created this super-chocolaty pie.

| | |
|---|---|
| 1 | *cup granulated sugar* |
| 3 | *tablespoons all-purpose flour* |
| 3 | *tablespoons cornstarch* |
| 3 | *cups milk, divided* |
| 3 | *large egg yolks, beaten* |
| 1½ | *teaspoons vanilla extract* |
| 3 | *ounces unsweetened chocolate, coarsely chopped* |
| 2 | *tablespoons unsalted butter* |
| ½ | *teaspoon salt* |
| 1 | *baked (9-inch) pie shell* |
| | *Sweetened whipped cream, for garnish (optional)* |

▪ In a medium bowl, whisk together the sugar, flour, and cornstarch. Sift the flour mixture and return it to the bowl. Gradually whisk in 1 cup of the milk, the egg yolks, and vanilla until smooth.

▪ In a large saucepan, combine the remaining 2 cups of milk, chocolate, butter, and salt. Over medium heat, stirring occasionally, bring the mixture just to a boil. Remove the pan from the heat. Gradually whisk about

1 cup of the hot chocolate-milk mixture into the bowl of yolk mixture until combined. Pour the mixture back into the saucepan and continue cooking, stirring frequently, until the mixture thickens and comes to a boil. Boil for 1 minute, stirring constantly.

▪ Pour the filling into the baked pie shell. Cover the surface of the filling with plastic wrap to prevent a skin from forming on top. Refrigerate the pie for 3 hours, or until thoroughly chilled. Garnish the pie with sweetened whipped cream, if desired.

*Makes 8 servings.*

# *I*SLAND *L*IME *P*IE

Island music heralded Chef Tell Erhardt's visit to "Live" from the Cayman Islands. He brought a little tropical flavor with him in the form of this pie. As well as operating his exclusive restaurant, Chef Tell's Grand Old House, in the Grand Cayman Islands, he also runs a catering service with two of his chefs in Tampa, Florida, called Chef Tell's Bayside Caterers.

| | |
|---|---|
| 1 | *envelope unflavored powdered gelatin* |
| 1 | *cup freshly squeezed lime juice, divided* |
| 1 | *teaspoon finely grated lime peel* |
| ¾ | *cup sweetened condensed milk* |
| | *Few drops of green food coloring (optional)* |
| 6 | *large egg whites* |
| 1 | *baked 9-inch pie shell* |
| ½ | *cup heavy cream* |
| 2 | *teaspoons granulated sugar* |
| | *Lime slices or grated lime peel, for garnish (optional)* |

▪ In a small heatproof cup, sprinkle the gelatin over ¼ cup of the lime juice. Let stand for 5 minutes, or until the gelatin is softened. Place the cup in a small saucepan with enough water to come halfway up the side of the cup. Heat the cup of gelatin in the water bath over medium-low heat, stirring constantly until the gelatin has dissolved. Remove the pan from the heat.

▪ In a large bowl, whisk together the remaining ¾ cup of lime juice, lime peel, sweetened condensed milk, and food coloring, if desired. Whisk in the gelatin mixture. In a large grease-free bowl, beat the egg whites with an electric mixer until soft peaks start to form. Fold the whites into the lime juice mixture. Pour the filling into the baked pie shell. Refrigerate for 2 hours, or until set.

▪ In a small bowl, beat the cream and sugar with an electric mixer until soft peaks start to form. Using a pastry bag, pipe a decoration on the pie with the whipped cream and garnish with lime slices or grated lime peel, if desired. Alternatively, serve each piece of pie with a dollop of cream and a slice of lime.

*Makes 8 servings.*

# CHEF PAUL PRUDHOMME'S INDIAN PUDDING

Asked which desserts she likes best, Kathie Lee answered that this recipe from frequent guest Chef Paul Prudhomme is one of her favorites. According to Chef Paul, early pioneers called almost anything made with corn or cornmeal "Indian" because corn was always known as Indian corn. Indian pudding is often made with molasses, but his version uses brown sugar. Toasted pine nuts add a genuinely Native American touch. Be sure to whip everything in the food processor until airy and then bake immediately for the lightest, most delicious results.

<sup></sup>

$\frac{1}{2}$   cup pine nuts

6   tablespoons unsalted butter

$\frac{3}{4}$   teaspoon ground allspice

$\frac{3}{4}$   teaspoon ground mace

$\frac{1}{2}$   cup plus 3 tablespoons firmly packed dark brown sugar

2   cans (12 ounces each) evaporated milk

$\frac{1}{2}$   teaspoon salt

2   medium eggs

1   teaspoon baking soda

1   teaspoon vanilla extract

1   cup yellow cornmeal

Heavy cream, for serving with the pudding (optional)

▪ Preheat the oven to 350° F.

▪ In a small skillet over medium heat, toast the pine nuts for about 3 minutes, or until light brown, stirring occasionally.

▪ In a small saucepan, melt the butter over high heat. When the butter begins to sizzle, stir in the allspice and mace and cook for 2 minutes, stirring constantly. Stir in the brown sugar and cook for about 30 seconds, or just until the sugar has dissolved. Add the evaporated milk and salt and cook, stirring occasionally, just until the milk is ready to boil. Remove the pan from the heat.

▪ In a food processor fitted with the metal chopping blade, process the eggs for about 25 seconds, or until very frothy. Add the baking soda and vanilla and process for 5 seconds longer. Add the cornmeal and process for about 40 seconds, until thoroughly blended. With the processor running, add the milk mixture in a steady stream and process for about 1 minute, or until thoroughly blended.

▪ Immediately pour the mixture into a 10-by-10-by-4-inch casserole. Sprinkle the toasted pine nuts evenly over the top and place the casserole in a large baking pan. Pour enough water into the pan to come about 1 inch up the side of the casserole. Bake 45 to 55 minutes, or until it is the consistency of pudding on top. Serve warm with heavy cream, if desired.

*Makes 6 to 8 servings.*

# GEORGIA PEACH BREAD PUDDING

Gerry Klaskala is the chef and managing partner of the Buckhead Diner in Atlanta, Georgia, one of the most respected restaurants in the United States. For his demonstration, he was asked to prepare a dish that is representative of the cuisine of the South. At his restaurant, in the heart of peach country, Gerry uses fresh Georgia peaches that have been poached; for ease of preparation at home, this version uses canned peaches.

| | |
|---|---|
| 1¾ | *cups granulated sugar, divided* |
| 1 | *pound bread, cut into 1-inch cubes* |
| 6 | *tablespoons butter, melted* |
| 2 | *cans (29 ounces each) sliced peaches in heavy syrup, drained* |
| 3 | *cups milk* |
| 6 | *large eggs* |
| 1 | *teaspoon ground cinnamon* |

■ Preheat the oven to 350° F. Lightly butter a 15-by-10-inch glass baking dish. Sprinkle with 1 tablespoon of the sugar. Set the dish aside.

■ Arrange the bread cubes on a jellyroll pan or a baking sheet. Drizzle the cubes with the melted butter and toss to coat. Bake for 15 to 20 minutes, or until the bread cubes are lightly toasted, stirring occasionally. Reduce the oven's temperature to 275° F.

■ Place the peaches from one can in a food processor fitted with a metal chopping blade and process until almost smooth.

■ In a large bowl, whisk together the milk, eggs, and ¾ cup of the sugar until blended. Stir in the peach puree and the peach slices from the second can. Stir in the bread cubes and then pour the mixture into the prepared dish. Sprinkle the top evenly with the remaining scant 1 cup of sugar and the cinnamon. Cover and bake for 60 to 75 minutes, or until set. Uncover for the last 15 to 20 minutes if you want the top to be crispier.

*Makes 12 to 16 servings.*

# HOMEMADE BANANA PUDDING

The Love Chef comes to the rescue again with a dessert that is wonderfully easy to make. This recipe is perfect for young children and equally appealing to anyone who is looking for comfort.

|  |  |
|---|---|
| ½ | cup granulated sugar, divided |
| 3 | tablespoons all-purpose flour |
|  | Dash of salt |
| 1 | whole large egg plus 3 large eggs, separated |
| 2 | cups milk |
| ½ | teaspoon vanilla extract |
| About 43 | vanilla wafer cookies |
| 4 to 5 | large ripe bananas, sliced into ¼-inch-thick slices (about 4 cups) |
|  | Additional sliced banana to garnish the top of the pudding (optional) |

▪ Preheat the oven to 425° F. Lightly butter a 2-quart deep baking dish (such as a soufflé dish).

▪ In the top pan of a double boiler, stir together ¼ cup plus 2 tablespoons of the sugar, the flour, and the salt. Whisk in the 1 whole egg plus the 3 egg yolks and the milk. Place the double boiler top pan over boiling water (the boiling water must be touching the bottom of the pan). Cook, whisking constantly, for about 10 minutes, or until the mixture has thickened. Remove the double boiler top from the lower pan. Whisk in the vanilla.

▪ Spoon ½ cup of the custard into the bottom of the prepared baking dish. Cover with a layer of cookies (about 8 to 10 cookies). Top the cookies with a layer of bananas. Spoon ⅔ cup of custard over the bananas. Cover the bananas with a layer of cookies. Arrange some of the cookies around the outside edge of the baking dish. Repeat with the remaining ingredients, ending with a layer of custard.

▪ In a medium grease-free bowl, using an electric mixer, beat the 3 egg whites until foamy. Gradually add the remaining 2 tablespoons of sugar and continue beating at high speed until stiff peaks begin to form.

▪ Spread the beaten egg whites in an even layer over the top of the last layer of custard. Bake the pudding for 5 minutes, or until the surface is lightly browned. Serve warm with additional banana slices, if desired.

*Makes 6 to 8 servings.*

# GERMAN APPLE CAKE

Chef Tell Erhardt prepared this delightful dish that would be a winner for brunch. The recipe, which came from his grandmother, has an easy-to-make crust that can also be used as a cookie dough and as a crust for fruit tarts.

### 1-2-3 DOUGH (enough for 2 crusts)

|       |                                           |
|-------|-------------------------------------------|
| 1     | *cup granulated sugar*                    |
| 1     | *large egg*                               |
| 2     | *cups (4 sticks) butter or margarine, softened* |
| 3     | *cups all-purpose flour*                  |

### APPLE CAKE FILLING

|         |                               |
|---------|-------------------------------|
| 4 to 5  | *large baking apples*         |
| 1/2     | *cup unseasoned bread crumbs* |
| 1       | *cup sour cream*              |
| 1/2     | *cup heavy cream*             |
| 1/2     | *cup granulated sugar*        |
| 2       | *large eggs*                  |
|         | *Juice of 1 lemon*            |
| 1       | *tablespoon cornstarch*       |
| 1/4     | *teaspoon vanilla extract*    |
| 1/2     | *cup apricot preserves*       |

- *To prepare the crust:* In a large bowl, combine the sugar, egg, butter, and flour. Using your fingertips, work the mixture together until it is of pastry consistency. Cover the dough and refrigerate for at least 1 hour, or until slightly firm.

- *To make the cake:* Preheat the oven to 375° F. Lightly butter a 9-inch springform pan. Dust lightly with flour and tap out any excess. Press half of the 1-2-3 Dough into the pan, covering the bottom and reaching about halfway up the sides. (Save the remaining dough for another use.)

- Peel the apples. Core, and cut them in half. Using the point of a small knife, cut small strips on top of the apples to score them.

- Sprinkle the bottom of the crust with the bread crumbs to form a thin, even layer. Arrange the apples, rounded side up, on the top. Fill in any empty spaces with pieces of apple.

- In a large bowl, stir together the sour cream, heavy cream, sugar, eggs, lemon juice, cornstarch, and vanilla. Pour this mixture over the apples. Bake for 60 to 90 minutes, or until the apples are tender and the filling is set.

- Remove the pan from the oven and set on a wire rack to cool. Cool completely before removing from the pan.

- In a small saucepan, heat the apricot preserves over medium heat until warm. When the cake has cooled slightly, brush the preserves over the top to form a glaze.

*Makes 6 to 8 servings plus leftover 1-2-3 Dough for another use.*

# THE CHOCOLATE DENSENESS

We've had decadences, indulgences, and death by chocolates; now we have The Denseness! This brownie-like cake is just as dense as its name implies. If you serve a wedge of it with the chocolate sauce recipe that follows, it's not really an overkill, but you might think that you died and went to heaven. Barbara Albright developed this recipe especially for

"Live." She was always expected to bring something rich and chocolatey wherever she went. Fortunately, this recipe is quick to make and freezes well. (To freeze The Denseness so that you always have one on hand, omit the sugar dusting and wrap the cake first in foil and then in plastic wrap.)

## "DENSENESS" CAKE

| | |
|---|---|
| 9 | ounces Swiss dark chocolate, coarsely chopped |
| 1 | cup all-purpose flour |
| 1/4 | teaspoon salt |
| 1/2 | cup (1 stick) unsalted butter, at room temperature |
| 1/3 | cup firmly packed brown sugar |
| 1/4 | cup granulated sugar |
| 2 | large eggs, at room temperature |
| 1 1/2 | teaspoons vanilla extract |
| 3/4 | cup finely chopped walnuts or pecans |
| | Confectioners' sugar, for dusting the top of the cake (optional) |
| | Walnut halves or chocolate-dipped walnut halves, for garnish (optional) |

## CHOCOLATE SAUCE

| | |
|---|---|
| 1/2 | cup plus 2 tablespoons heavy (whipping) cream |
| | A few grains of salt |
| 5 | ounces Swiss dark chocolate, finely chopped |
| 1/2 | teaspoon vanilla extract |

▪ Position a rack in the center of the oven and preheat to 350° F. Butter the bottom and side of an 8-by-2-inch round cake pan. Line the bottom of the pan with a circle of baking parchment or waxed paper. Dust the side of the pan with flour and tap out the excess.

▪ *To make the cake:* Melt the chocolate (see Box) and cool for 5 to 10 minutes, or until tepid. In a small bowl, stir together the flour and salt.

▪ In a large bowl, using a hand-held electric mixer set at medium speed, beat the butter with the sugars for 30 to 40 seconds, or until creamy. One at a time, beat in the eggs, beating well after each addition. Beat in the chocolate and vanilla. At low speed, mix in the flour mixture, just until combined. Stir in the nuts.

▪ Scrape the batter into the prepared pan and smooth the top with a rubber spatula. Bake the cake for 30 to 35 minutes, or until a cake tester or toothpick inserted 2 inches away from the center comes out with a few moist crumbs clinging to it. Do not overbake.

▪ Transfer the cake in the pan to a wire rack to cool for 15 minutes. Run a knife around the edge of the cake to loosen it from the pan and invert it onto the wire rack. Carefully peel off the paper and leave it loosely set on the bottom of the cake. Cool completely. Dust the top of the cake with confectioners' sugar and garnish with walnut halves, if desired.

▪ *To make the sauce:* In a small saucepan, bring the heavy cream and salt to a gentle boil. Stir in the chocolate and remove from the heat. Let the mixture stand for 2 minutes to melt the chocolate. Whisk until smooth. Stir in the vanilla.

*Makes 8 servings with approximately ¾ cup sauce.*

## How To Melt Chocolate

Melting chocolate requires gentle heat. Chocolate that is overheated may scorch, lose its flavor, or turn coarse and grainy. A microwave oven can melt chocolate quickly and easily. You can also use the conventional double-boiler method.

**In a microwave oven:** Place coarsely chopped chocolate in a microwave-safe container and microwave at Medium (50 percent) for 1½ to 4 minutes, until the chocolate turns shiny. In the microwave, chocolate maintains its shape even after it has melted, so make sure to give it a stir just to check. Remove the container from the microwave and stir the chocolate until completely melted.

Stir milk and white chocolates after about 1½ minutes. Because of their milk proteins, they need to be stirred sooner than dark chocolate. (If overheated, these chocolates may become grainy.)

**In a double boiler:** Place coarsely chopped chocolate in the top of a double boiler over hot, not simmering, water. Melt the chocolate, stirring until smooth. Remove the top part of the double boiler from the bottom. (Don't let the water boil as the steam may cause the chocolate to "seize" and become grainy.)

# White Chocolate Cheesecake

Chef Tell Erhardt, up from his Grand Old House restaurant in the Grand Cayman Islands, demonstrated this equally grand cheesecake.

### CHEESECAKE

8    *ounces white chocolate (such as Lindt), coarsely chopped*
2    *pounds cream cheese, at room temperature*
1    *cup granulated sugar*
4    *large eggs, at room temperature*
1    *teaspoon vanilla extract*

### RASPBERRY SAUCE

2    *cups unsweetened frozen raspberries, thawed*
1    *cup granulated sugar*
½    *cup framboise (clear raspberry brandy), divided*

■ *To make the cheesecake:* Preheat the oven to 250° F. Lightly butter a 10-inch springform pan. Line the bottom of the pan with aluminum foil.

■ In the top of a double boiler, over hot, not simmering, water, melt the white chocolate. If you prefer, you can melt the white chocolate in a microwave-safe bowl in the microwave on medium power, stirring until the chocolate is smooth. (Take care: white chocolate scorches easily.)

■ In a large bowl, using an electric mixer, beat the cream cheese until smooth. Add the sugar and beat on medium-high until combined. One at a time, beat in the eggs, scraping the sides of the bowl after each addition. Beat in the vanilla and the melted white chocolate. Scrape the batter into the prepared pan and shake gently to level the mixture.

■ Set the pan inside a larger pan and pour boiling water into the outer pan to a depth of about 1 inch. Set the pans on the center rack in the oven and bake for about 70 minutes, or until the center springs back when lightly touched.

▪ Remove the cheesecake pan from the water bath and cool on a wire rack. Cover the cheesecake and refrigerate for 6 hours, or until cold.

▪ *To make the sauce:* In a blender, process the raspberries, sugar, and framboise until smooth. Strain the raspberry sauce to remove the seeds. Store the sauce, covered, in the refrigerator.

▪ To serve, loosen the cake from the side of the springform pan by running a thin-bladed knife around the edge. Snap open the springform and remove the side and bottom of the pan. Slice the cake with a long knife that has been dipped in hot water and wiped dry. Serve with the raspberry sauce spooned over each slice.

*Makes 12 servings.*

# CHOCOLATE OBLIVION TRUFFLE TORTE

Rose Levy Beranbaum, author of several books on desserts, chose this recipe from *The Cake Bible* to prepare on "Live" because it is absolutely the most delicious way she knows of to eat chocolate. She even recalled a time on a visit to her brother, who did not possess a cake pan but who shared her craving for chocolate, when she improvised and made the cake in a saucepan! On the show, however, Regis refused to take a bite of Rose's decadent delight until she had checked out the status of his washboard "abs" from his latest exercise program. In the end, both he and Kathie Lee succumbed and sampled this gooey treat. Rose prefers to serve this torte at room temperature and says it is fabulous with sweetened whipped cream.

5⅓   *bars (3 ounces each) bittersweet chocolate*
1   *cup (2 sticks) unsalted butter, softened*
6   *large eggs, at room temperature*

■ Preheat the oven to 425° F. Butter an 8-inch springform pan and line the bottom with buttered baking parchment or waxed paper. Wrap the outside of the pan with a double layer of heavy-duty foil to prevent any seepage.

■ In a large metal bowl set over a pan of hot, not simmering, water (the bottom of the bowl should not touch the water), combine the chocolate and butter and let stand, stirring occasionally, until smooth and melted.

■ In another large metal bowl set over a pan of simmering water, heat the eggs until just warm to the touch, stirring constantly to prevent curdling. Remove the bowl from the heat and beat until the eggs have tripled in volume and soft peaks form when the beater is raised. If you are using a heavy-duty mixer with a whisk beater, this will take about 5 minutes. If you are using a hand-held electric mixer, beat the eggs over the simmering water until they are hot to the touch, about 5 minutes. Remove the bowl from the heat and continue beating the eggs until they are cool.

■ Using a large wire whisk or a rubber spatula, fold half of the eggs into the chocolate mixture until they are almost incorporated. Fold in the remaining eggs just until blended and no streaks remain. Finish by using a rubber spatula to ensure that the heavier mixture at the bottom is fully incorporated. Scrape the batter into the prepared pan and smooth the surface with the spatula. Set the pan in a larger pan and fill the larger pan with enough very hot water so that it comes 1 inch up the side of the smaller pan.

■ Bake for 5 minutes. Cover the surface loosely with a piece of buttered foil and bake for 10 minutes longer. (The cake will look soft.) Remove the springform pan to a wire rack and allow the cake to cool for 45 minutes. Cover with plastic wrap and refrigerate for 3 hours, or until thoroughly chilled.

■ To unmold the torte, have ready a serving plate and also a flat plate, at least 8 inches in diameter, covered with plastic wrap. Wipe around the outside of the pan with a hot damp towel.

■ Run a thin metal spatula around the side of the torte and release the sides of the springform pan. Place the plastic-wrapped plate on top and invert. Wipe the bottom of the pan with a hot damp towel. Remove the bottom of the pan and the parchment. Reinvert the torte onto the serving plate. Cut into thin slices to serve. The torte will store in the refrigerator for up to 2 weeks, but it does not freeze well.

*Makes 16 servings.*

# *P*AN DE JEREZ
## (CHOCOLATE SHERRY TORTE)

Joyce Goldstein, chef and owner of the highly acclaimed San Francisco Square One Restaurant, prepared this recipe from her book, *The Mediterranean Kitchen*. The version that follows uses sherry, but this dense and delicious cake is also good made with port. Regis's contribution to Joyce's segment was to get over-enthusiastic with the electric mixer and splatter whipped cream all over the set.

| | |
|---|---|
| 11 | tablespoons unsalted butter |
| ½ | cup sherry |
| 4½ | ounces bittersweet chocolate, coarsely chopped |
| 2 | ounces unsweetened chocolate, coarsely chopped |
| 2 | tablespoons amaretto liqueur |
| 5 | large eggs, separated |
| ¾ | cup granulated sugar |
| 2 | teaspoons vanilla extract |
| | Pinch of salt |
| ⅓ | cup sifted cake flour |
| | Sweetened whipped cream or custard sauce, for serving with the torte (optional) |

▪ Place the butter, sherry, both chocolates, and amaretto in the top of a double boiler. Heat over hot, not simmering, water, until melted and smooth, stirring frequently. Let cool to room temperature.

▪ Preheat the oven to 350° F. Butter a 9-by-5-inch loaf pan and line the bottom of the pan with baking parchment.

▪ In a large bowl, using an electric mixer, beat the egg yolks and ½ cup of the sugar until the mixture forms a slowly dissolving ribbon when the beaters are lifted.

▪ In another large grease-free bowl, beat the egg whites until foamy. Gradually beat in the remaining ¼ cup of sugar and continue to beat until soft peaks start to form. Stir the cooled chocolate mixture, the vanilla, and the salt into the egg-yolk mixture. Sift the flour over the batter. Add the egg whites and fold them in just until the mixture is combined.

■ Pour the batter into the prepared pan and smooth the surface. Place the pan in a larger baking pan. Add enough hot water so that it comes 2 inches up the side of the loaf pan. (This is a water bath.) Cover both pans tightly with aluminum foil. Bake for 40 to 50 minutes, or just until a toothpick inserted into the cake's center comes out clean (do not over-bake).

■ Remove the loaf pan from the water bath and let the cake cool in the pan. Run a knife around the sides of the pan and turn the cake out onto a serving platter. If the cake sticks, warm the pan slightly over very low heat on the stove top. Cut the loaf into 1-inch-thick slices. Serve with sweetened whipped cream or custard sauce, if desired.

*Makes 9 servings.*

Steve Friedman/Buena Vista Television

*Here's looking at you, kid.*

# AUNT PITTYPAT'S PECAN POUND CAKE

This cake recipe was chosen for the gala at Radio City Music Hall celebrating the 50th anniversary of *Gone With the Wind*. The recipe's creator, Lynne Tolley, is the proprietor of Miss Mary Bobo's Boarding House, a Southern regional restaurant in Lynchburg, Tennessee. Almost everyone is amazed that Lynne can run a successful restaurant in a town with a population of 361! Fortunately, 250,000 visitors a year come to Lynchburg to visit the oldest registered distillery in the United States—the Jack Daniel distillery. And Lynne is the great-grandniece of its founder, Jack Daniel.

## PECAN POUND CAKE

| | |
|---|---|
| 3 | cups sifted cake flour |
| 2 | teaspoons baking powder |
| 1 | teaspoon salt |
| 1/2 | teaspoon freshly grated nutmeg |
| 1 | cup (2 sticks) unsalted butter, softened |
| 2 1/2 | cups granulated sugar |
| 6 | large eggs, at room temperature |
| 1 | cup sour cream, at room temperature |
| 1/2 | cup Jack Daniel's Whiskey |
| 1 | cup finely chopped pecans |

## GONE WITH THE WIND GLAZE

| | |
|---|---|
| 2 | cups confectioners' sugar |
| 1 | tablespoon Jack Daniel's Whiskey |
| 1 to 3 | tablespoons water |
| | Confectioners' sugar, for dusting the top of the cake (optional) |

■ *To make the cake:* Preheat the oven to 325° F. Lightly butter a 10-inch tube pan or a bundt cake pan, making sure to butter the center tube. Dust with flour and tap out any excess.

■ In a large bowl, stir together the flour, baking powder, salt, and nutmeg, then sift the mixture.

■ In a large bowl, using an electric mixer set at medium-high speed, beat the butter until smooth and creamy. Gradually beat in the sugar and continue beating for 2 to 5 minutes, or until the mixture is light and almost white in color. One at a time, beat in the eggs, beating well after each addition and scraping down the side of the bowl.

■ On low speed, beat in the flour mixture, one-third at a time, alternating it with the sour cream and the whiskey. (You should begin and end with the flour mixture.) Scrape down the side of the bowl and mix in the pecans.

■ Scrape the batter into the prepared pan and bake for 70 to 75 minutes, or until a cake tester or toothpick inserted into the center of the cake comes out clean. Transfer the cake in the pan to a wire rack to cool for 15 minutes. Invert the cake onto the rack and leave to cool completely.

■ *To make the glaze:* In a medium bowl, stir together the sugar, whiskey, and enough water to make a pourable mixture. Whisk until very smooth.

■ Pour the glaze over the cooled cake. Or, if you prefer, dust the top of the cake with confectioners' sugar just before serving.

*Makes 12 to 16 servings.*

## WHAT DOES CODY LIKE TO EAT?

**KATHIE LEE:** Anything that we call pizza, Cody will eat! We are really very basic eaters. Cody loves meatloaf, and he loves it when his daddy cooks for him. (He doesn't know that Mommy actually knows how to cook, too.) Also, Cody loves "mashers" —that's what we call mashed potatoes—and corn on the cob. Even when I take the corn off the cob for him, he whines, "Mommy, I want your corn!" Then he leaves his little teeth marks on my cob of corn.

# JOSEPH'S KNOCKOUT CARROT CAKE

Joseph C. Phillips, a costar on "The Cosby Show," appeared on "Live" during a week that featured bachelors who cook. He selected this recipe from his repertoire because "it's the best carrot cake I've ever tasted." Joseph's demonstration was moved to later in the show, which made him late for a dress rehearsal for "The Cosby Show" and earned him a reprimand from the show's director, Jay Sandrich. They made up, however, as soon as Joseph gave him a slice of his cake.

This cake is also excellent left unfrosted and sprinkled with a dusting of confectioners' sugar just before serving. Sandwich any leftover icing between graham crackers to make some mouth-watering cookies.

### CARROT CAKE

| | |
|---|---|
| 1 | cup sifted all-purpose flour |
| 1 | teaspoon baking soda |
| $\frac{1}{2}$ | teaspoon salt |
| 2 | large eggs |
| 1 | cup granulated sugar |
| $\frac{3}{4}$ | cup vegetable oil |
| 1 | tablespoon vanilla extract |
| 1 | teaspoon ground cinnamon |
| $\frac{1}{2}$ | teaspoon freshly grated nutmeg |
| 5 | small raw carrots, peeled and grated |
| 1 | can (8 ounces) crushed pineapple in unsweetened pineapple juice, thoroughly drained (about $\frac{3}{4}$ cup) |
| $\frac{1}{2}$ | cup chopped walnuts |

### CREAM CHEESE ICING

| | |
|---|---|
| 8 | ounces cream cheese, at room temperature |
| $\frac{1}{2}$ | cup (1 stick) butter, at room temperature |
| $1\frac{1}{2}$ | teaspoons vanilla extract |
| 4 | cups sifted confectioners' sugar |

▪ *To make the cake:* Preheat the oven to 350° F. Lightly butter a 9-inch round cake pan. Dust with flour and tap out the excess.

▪ Sift together the flour, baking soda, and salt, and set it aside.

▪ In a large bowl, using an electric mixer, beat together the eggs and sugar until light yellow. With the mixer set on low, add the oil, vanilla, cinnamon, and nutmeg. Add the flour mixture, mixing until well blended. Using a wooden spoon, stir in the carrots, pineapple, and walnuts.

▪ Spoon the mixture into the prepared pan. Bake for 40 to 45 minutes, or until a toothpick inserted into the center of the cake comes out clean. Transfer the cake in the pan to a wire rack to cool for 15 minutes. Run a knife around the edge of the cake to loosen it from the pan and invert it onto the rack. Cool completely.

▪ *To make the glaze:* In a large bowl, using an electric mixer, beat the cream cheese and butter together just until smooth. Beat in the vanilla. Gradually beat in the confectioners' sugar until smooth. Be careful not to overbeat the icing or it will become too soft. Frost the cake and store it in the refrigerator.

*Makes 8 to 12 servings.*

## WHAT ARE THE FUNNIEST THINGS THAT HAVE HAPPENED DURING A FOOD SEGMENT?

**REGIS, KATHIE LEE, AND GELMAN:** One time there was a little boy on the show who had won a cooking contest. When it came time to taste his winning recipe, his response was, "I'm not tasting it. I don't eat that stuff." Another time, there were some Playboy Club bunnies on the show. There was a fire on the stove in the stage kitchen. While everyone ran for safety, Regis ran for a bunny and saved her!

# CHOCOLATE TURTLE COOKIES

These sumptuous cookies are sold at The Golden Pear, a charming specialty foods and coffee shop just blocks away from the most elite seacoast real estate in Southampton, New York. The cookies were featured in *Chocolatier* magazine, and editor-in-chief Barbara Albright was on "Live" to demonstrate this chocolaty treat.

| | |
|---|---|
| ½ | cup all-purpose flour |
| ½ | teaspoon baking powder |
| ¼ | teaspoon salt |
| 1½ | tablespoons instant espresso powder |
| 2 | teaspoons vanilla extract |
| 12 | ounces semisweet chocolate, coarsely chopped |
| 4 | ounces unsweetened chocolate, coarsely chopped |
| ¼ | cup (½ stick) unsalted butter, cut into 4 pieces |
| 1½ | cups granulated sugar, divided |
| 4 | large eggs, lightly beaten (at room temperature) |
| 2 | cups coarsely chopped walnuts or pecans |
| 12 | ounces (about 2 cups) semisweet chocolate chips |
| 2 | cups pecan halves, for decoration |

▪ Preheat the oven to 350° F. Line 2 baking sheets with baking parchment or aluminum foil.

▪ In a medium bowl, stir together the flour, baking powder, and salt. In a small cup, dissolve the espresso powder in the vanilla extract.

▪ In the top of a double boiler over hot, not simmering, water, melt the coarsely chopped chocolates with the butter, stirring frequently until smooth. Transfer the chocolate mixture to a large bowl. Using a wire whisk, stir in ½ cup of the sugar. Gradually stir in the eggs. Mix in the remaining 1 cup of sugar and the espresso-vanilla mixture. Stir in the flour mixture. Stir in the chopped nuts and the chocolate chips.

▪ Using a ¼-cup measuring cup, drop the dough onto the prepared baking sheets, leaving about 2 inches between cookies. Insert 5 pecan halves around the bottom of each cookie to represent the "turtle's" 4 legs and head. Bake the cookies, 1 baking sheet at a time, for 10 to 12 minutes, or until the cookies' tops start to crack. Do not overbake; the cookies should be soft and fudgy. Cool the cookies on the sheets, set on a wire rack. Store in an airtight container for up to 5 days. These cookies freeze well.

*Makes about 24 cookies.*

# Merveilles

Jean-Louis Palladin has been rated as one of the finest chefs in North America. He is the owner of Jean-Louis at the Watergate Hotel in Washington, D.C., and the author of a gorgeous book, *Jean-Louis: Cooking with the Seasons*. These delicate pastry cookies are fried, then lightly dusted with confectioners' sugar—and they will melt in your mouth.

| | |
|---|---|
| 2 | *cups all-purpose flour* |
| ½ | *teaspoon baking powder* |
| | *Pinch of salt* |
| 2 | *large eggs, at room temperature* |
| 2 | *tablespoons granulated sugar* |
| ¼ | *cup (½ stick) butter, softened* |
| ½ | *teaspoon finely grated lemon peel* |
| 1 | *tablespoon brandy* |
| | *Vegetable oil, for frying* |
| | *Confectioners' sugar, for dusting the cookies* |

▪ In a medium bowl, stir together the flour, baking powder, and salt. Sift the flour mixture.

# *Let's Celebrate*

# NEW YEAR'S TRIFLE

Joanna Pruess, author of *The Supermarket Epicure* and creator of a cooking school in a major supermarket chain, appeared on "Live" just before New Year's Eve. She was asked to prepare something very festive and special for the event, but to make it also a dish that could be done ahead of time. She chose this recipe for trifle. Trifles have been a favorite English dessert since the days of the first Queen Elizabeth; Queen Victoria, too, was particularly fond of trifle.

|          |                                          |
| -------- | ---------------------------------------- |
| 2        | cups eggnog                              |
| 16 to 20 | ladyfingers                              |
| ¾        | cup sweet sherry                         |
| 2        | ounces slivered almonds, toasted         |
| 1        | cup raspberry preserves                  |
| 2        | cups mixed fruit or fruit cocktail, drained |
|          | Crushed amaretti cookies to cover the surface |
| 1 to 2   | cups heavy cream                         |
| 1½       | tablespoons granulated sugar             |

■ Pour the eggnog into the bottom of a 2½-quart serving bowl.

■ Arrange the ladyfingers over the eggnog and against the sides of the dish. Moisten the ladyfingers with the sherry.

■ Sprinkle the almonds evenly over the ladyfingers. Spoon the preserves evenly over the surface. Distribute the mixed fruit over the top. Sprinkle the surface with the amaretti cookies. Cover and refrigerate until ready to serve.

■ In a large bowl, using an electric mixer, beat the cream and the sugar until soft peaks start to form. Using a pastry bag, pipe a decorative top on the trifle, or simply spoon the whipped cream over the top.

*Makes 8 to 10 servings.*

# EASTER ROAST LEG OF LAMB WITH SCALLIONS AND POTATOES

Chef Stefano Battistini, now of that quintessential New York City establishment, The Four Seasons, made this very traditional Easter recipe for the viewers of "Live." It's a splendid way to celebrate the arrival of spring. Serve it with a light red wine and an assortment of fresh spring vegetables.

| | |
|---|---|
| 1 | leg of lamb (6 to 8 pounds), trimmed of visible fat |
| 12 | small garlic cloves |
| 12 | small sprigs of rosemary |
| 2 | teaspoons salt |
| 2 | teaspoons coarsely ground black pepper |
| ¼ | cup olive oil |
| 2 | pounds small potatoes, well scrubbed |
| 1 | pound scallions |
| 2 | cups dry white wine |
| 1 | tablespoon prepared mustard |

■ Using the point of a small sharp knife, cut 12 slits in the leg of lamb. Insert a garlic clove and a rosemary sprig in each slit.

■ Rub the lamb all over with the salt, pepper, and oil. Cover and refrigerate overnight.

■ Preheat the oven to 400° F.

■ Place the lamb in a roasting pan. Roast for 25 minutes, then add the vegetables. Continue cooking the lamb for 25 to 40 minutes longer, or until the lamb is done to your liking. (Remove the vegetables if they are getting overcooked.) Transfer the lamb to a cutting board.

■ Remove and discard excess fat from the pan drippings. Place the roasting pan on the stove top and add the wine. Cook over high heat and boil until the mixture is slightly thickened, scraping up the browned bits from the bottom. Stir in the mustard to finish the sauce.

▪ Remove the garlic cloves and rosemary before carving the lamb. Serve the lamb with the sauce and vegetables.

*Makes 8 to 12 servings.*

# GAELTACH CHICKEN

Eamonn Doran is more than the founder of three New York City restaurants—he is a warm and welcoming social chairman and host to anyone who is Irish or wishes he or she were Irish. Patrons at his restaurants tend to become friends with each other, because Eamonn and the bartenders introduce everyone in the bar area. In fact, customers have taken group trips to Ireland!

Eamonn's and wife Clare's American dream began in February 1977 at 998 Second Avenue. With lots of Irish luck, his group is still going strong. Christian Dubrevil, a Parisian friend of Eamonn's, opened a second Eamonn Doran's near Madison Square Garden on St. Patrick's Day in 1988. In 1991, Clare opened her own Eamonn Doran's in the Eastgate Towers Hotel.

So who better than Eamonn to appear on "Live" on St. Patrick's Day with this special recipe that Clare received from Eamonn's mother?

| | |
|---|---|
| 1 | *roasting chicken (4 to 5 pounds)* |
| ½ | *orange* |
| 1 | *onion, divided* |
| 2 | *tablespoons melted butter, margarine, or oil* |
| ½ | *cup milk* |
| 3 | *large slices crustless white bread* |
| 2 | *tablespoons chopped parsley* |
| 1 | *teaspoon chopped fresh thyme leaves or ½ teaspoon dried thyme leaves, crushed* |
| | *Liver of the chicken, chopped* |
| | *Pinch of ground nutmeg* |
| | *Salt and pepper to taste* |

▪ Preheat the oven to 350° F. Butter a small casserole dish.

▪ Peel and cut the onion in half. Place one half with the orange half into the body of the chicken and secure the chicken closed with a skewer.

▪ Place the chicken in a roasting pan and rub the butter, margarine, or oil over the breast and legs. Sprinkle with salt, if you wish. Cover the chicken with foil and roast for no longer than 1½ hours.

▪ Meanwhile, make the stuffing. Pour the milk into a bowl. Add the bread slices and soak until moistened. (Don't let it get too wet.) Pour off any extra milk. Chop up the remaining onion half and add it and the rest of the ingredients to the softened bread. Mix thoroughly. Season with salt and pepper. Place the stuffing in the prepared dish and bake for 1 hour along with the chicken.

*Makes 6 to 8 servings.*

# *F*IGHTING *I*RISH *F*LAMBÉ

On the first of The Clever Cleaver Brothers' many appearances on "Live with Regis & Kathie Lee" they made this dessert in keeping with Regis's passion for Notre Dame and the fact that their appearance coincided with St. Patrick's Day. The Cleavers have their own half-hour cooking show in Southern California, but they were excited about their national debut. Clad in tuxedos, they identified themselves as follows:

> We're The Clever Cleavers, and we're here to say
> We get into food in an intimate way,
> But don't get us wrong 'cause we really don't mean
> To give you the impression that we're talking obscene.
> It's just that food is our livelihood,
> So we know how to cook the way that others *wish* they could.

2  tablespoons butter
2  cups sliced fresh strawberries
2  tablespoons granulated sugar
¼  cup currants
¼  cup walnuts
   Few dashes of aromatic bitters
2  tablespoons Irish Mist liqueur
½  cup Irish Cream liqueur
   Pinch of ground cinnamon
   Pinch of grated nutmeg
2  cups vanilla ice cream
   Sweetened whipped cream, for topping the dessert

▪ In a large skillet, heat the butter over medium heat. Add the strawberries and sprinkle them evenly with the sugar. Gently toss the strawberries until coated evenly with the mixture and cook for just 15 to 30 seconds. *Do not overcook.*

▪ Add the currants, walnuts, and bitters. Remove the pan from the heat and add the Irish Mist. Flame the strawberries by touching the liqueur with a lighted match. When the flame has died down, stir in the Irish Cream, cinnamon, and nutmeg. Heat over low heat until the mixture thickens slightly.

▪ Place scoops of the ice cream in 4 dessert dishes. Top with the strawberry mixture and a dollop of whipped cream.

*Makes 4 servings.*

## WHAT HOLIDAY MEALS WERE YOUR FAVORITES?

**KATHIE LEE:** When I was a child, Mom would cook the Thanksgiving turkey overnight—very slowly—so that when we woke up in the morning, it was practically falling off the bone, and the whole house would smell of the turkey. That night before was a big preparation, and I was my mother's sous chef. I'd cut all the celery and onions and would look like I was sobbing—but, you know, I didn't mind for Thanksgiving.

*Steve Friedman/Buena Vista Television*

*Jack O'Lantern glares as Regis makes a point.*

# *T*HANKFUL RICE

Here is a great recipe from Francis Anthony, the Love Chef, for a rice dressing you can use to stuff your Thanksgiving bird or to offer alongside it. (We've given directions here for serving the dressing on the side.)

|  |  |
|---|---|
| 3 | tablespoons olive oil |
| 2 | cups chopped scallions |
| 1½ | cups chopped celery |
| 3 | cups slightly undercooked brown rice |
| 3 | cups slightly undercooked white rice |
| 1 | jar (2 ounces) sliced pimientos |
| 2 | tablespoons toasted pine nuts |

1     cup chicken broth
1½    tablespoons freshly squeezed lemon juice
2     teaspoons poultry seasoning
½     teaspoon ground coriander
¼     teaspoon freshly ground black pepper
      Salt to taste

■ In a large skillet, heat the oil over medium-high heat. Add the scallions and celery and cook for 8 to 12 minutes, or until the vegetables are softened slightly but not browned.

■ Remove the skillet from the heat and stir in the brown and white rice, pimientos, and pine nuts. In a medium bowl, stir together the broth, lemon juice, poultry seasoning, coriander, pepper, and salt.

■ Pour the seasoned broth over the rice mixture and toss gently to mix. Spoon the mixture into a baking dish and cover with a lid or aluminum foil. Bake in the oven at 325° F. for 45 minutes (during the last hour of the turkey roasting time).

*Makes 15 to 18 servings.*

# CHRISTMAS PUNCH

While its maker, the Love Chef, calls this a Christmas punch, it would be equally appropriate in the summer. Ahead of time, freeze water or lemonade in a ring mold to make the ice ring for this nonalcoholic punch. For a specially festive touch, you could place whole strawberries in the ring before adding the liquid and freezing.

1    pint fresh strawberries, cleaned and hulled
4    quarts seltzer water
1    can (6 ounces) frozen lemonade
1    can (6 ounces) frozen grapefruit juice
3    dashes of bitters
     Ice cubes or an ice ring

- In the container of a blender, process the strawberries until pureed.

- In a large punch bowl, combine the pureed strawberries with the seltzer, lemonade, grapefruit juice, and bitters. Add ice cubes or an ice ring.

*Makes 24 to 30 servings.*

# THE POLAR BREEZE

Love Chef Francis Anthony demonstrated this refreshing and potent beverage that just suits holiday get-togethers. Candy canes make perfect swizzle sticks. (This recipe is easily doubled.)

|           |                                      |
|-----------|--------------------------------------|
| 1½        | *ounces brandy*                      |
| 1         | *ounce peppermint schnapps*          |
| About ½   | *cup of crushed ice*                 |
|           | *Candy cane, to use as a swizzle stick* |

*For a little extra yuletide cheer, Kathie Lee sings a holiday song.*

Steve Friedman/Buena Vista Television

▪ In a shaker, combine the brandy, schnapps, and ice and shake for about 5 seconds. Strain the liquid into a chilled cocktail glass and serve with a candy cane swizzle stick.

*Makes 1 serving.*

# KENTUCKY CHRISTMAS HAM

When the gang's all in for the holidays, the Love Chef comes to the rescue with a very special recipe for ham. Use whatever kind or brand of ham you like best.

| | |
|---|---|
| 1 | *ham (12 to 14 pounds)* |
| 3/4 | *cup bourbon* |
| 2 | *cups firmly packed dark brown sugar* |
| 1 | *tablespoon orange marmalade* |
| 1 | *tablespoon dry mustard* |
| 1/8 | *teaspoon ground coriander seed* |
| | *Whole cloves for garnish (optional)* |

▪ Bake the ham as directed. Remove the ham from the oven about 30 minutes before it is done. Increase the oven temperature to 450° F.

▪ If the ham has a rind, once it is cool enough to handle, cut away the rind and trim the fat to about ½ inch thick. Score by cutting deeply in a crisscross pattern.

▪ Using a pastry brush, brush bourbon all over the ham. In a small bowl, stir together the remaining bourbon, brown sugar, marmalade, mustard, and coriander. Pat the mixture firmly all over the ham. Stud the ham with the cloves, if desired. Return the ham to the oven for 30 minutes longer.

*Makes 20 to 24 servings.*

# ROAST CHRISTMAS GOOSE

As a change of pace from turkey or ham, try Chef Tell's recipe for goose this Christmas. It's different—and delicious—but harder to carve than turkey. Don't try to slice more than the breast and thigh meat at table; goose is so rich that smaller portions are in order. You can take the carcass apart later, in the kitchen, for leftovers.

|        |                                     |
|--------|-------------------------------------|
| 1      | (10- to 14-pound) young goose       |
|        | Salt and pepper to taste            |
| 5 to 6 | sprigs of rosemary                  |
| 6      | sprigs of thyme                     |
| 2      | apples, cut into quarters           |
| 2      | oranges, cut into quarters          |
| 2      | onions, peeled and cut into quarters|

▪ Preheat the oven to 375° F.

▪ Sprinkle the goose with salt and pepper, both inside and out. Remove any additional fat and discard. Prick the skin to allow the fat beneath to run out as it cooks. Place the rosemary and thyme in the cavity.

▪ Place the goose, breast side down, in a deep roasting pan. Arrange the apples, oranges, and onions around the goose in the pan. Pour in enough water to come halfway up the sides of the goose.

▪ Roast for 2 to 2½ hours. Pour off the fat from time to time and add more water if necessary, stirring it into the pan juices.

▪ Turn the goose breast side up and roast for 1½ to 2 hours longer, or until completely cooked (180° F on a meat thermometer, inserted in the meaty inner thigh). Pour off the fat and add more water as necessary, stirring it into the pan juices.

▪ Transfer the goose to a large serving platter and keep it warm. Remove any remaining fat from the sauce. Strain the sauce and season with salt and pepper. Serve the goose with the sauce.

*Makes 10 to 15 servings.*

# *H*OLIDAY *S*WEET *P*OTATO *P*ECAN *P*IES

Model Barbara Smith appeared on "Live" to demonstrate this best-selling dessert from her stylish New York City restaurant. Located in the theater district, B. Smith's features jazz musicians and is a popular place to go before or after seeing a Broadway play. Sweet potatoes are often thought of as a homey food, but there is nothing humble about these elegant small pies.

## PIE CRUST

| | |
|---|---|
| 4 | *cups all-purpose flour* |
| ³/₄ | *cup granulated sugar* |
| 1 | *teaspoon salt* |
| 1 | *teaspoon ground cinnamon* |
| ¹/₂ | *teaspoon ground cloves* |
| ¹/₂ | *teaspoon grated nutmeg* |
| 1 | *cup (2 sticks) cold butter, cut into 1-inch pieces* |
| 4 | *large eggs, lightly beaten* |

## NUT MIXTURE

| | |
|---|---|
| 1 | *cup finely ground pecans* |
| ¹/₂ | *cup light corn syrup* |
| ¹/₄ | *cup (¹/₂ stick) unsalted butter, melted and cooled* |

SWEET POTATO FILLING

| | |
|---|---|
| 1 | pound sweet potatoes or yams, peeled and cut into cubes |
| 1/2 | cup all-purpose flour |
| 1/2 | cup plus 2 tablespoons granulated sugar |
| 6 | tablespoons firmly packed brown sugar |
| 2 | teaspoons grated nutmeg |
| 1 | teaspoon ground cinnamon |
| 1/4 | teaspoon ground allspice |
| 1/2 | cup plus 2 tablespoons heavy cream |
| 2 | large eggs |
| 2 | tablespoons brandy |
| 1/4 | cup (1/2 stick) unsalted butter or margarine, melted and cooled Pecan halves, for decorating the top of each pie |

▪ *To make the pie crust:* In a food processor fitted with the metal chopping blade, combine the flour, sugar, salt, cinnamon, cloves, and nutmeg. Add the butter to the processor and pulse until the mixture resembles coarse cornmeal. Add the eggs and process until a ball of dough forms. Divide the dough into 8 balls. Flatten each ball slightly into a disk. Wrap and refrigerate.

▪ *To make the nut mixture:* In a medium bowl, stir together the pecans, syrup, and butter until combined. Cover and refrigerate overnight.

▪ *To prepare the tart shells:* On a lightly floured surface, using a lightly floured rolling pin, roll out each piece of dough so that it is a scant 1/4 inch thick. Press the pieces of dough into six 4½-inch tart pans and freeze for 60 minutes.

▪ *To make the sweet potato filling:* In a large saucepan over high heat, bring the sweet potatoes and enough water to cover them to a boil. Reduce the heat to low, cover, and simmer for 15 to 20 minutes, or until the potatoes are soft. Drain the potatoes.

▪ In a large bowl, beat the potatoes with an electric mixer until they are smooth. Beat in the flour, granulated sugar, brown sugar, nutmeg, cinnamon, and allspice. Add the cream, eggs, and brandy and beat for about 1 minute, or until light and creamy. At low speed, beat in the butter.

▪ Preheat the oven to 350° F.

▪ *To assemble the pies:* Divide the nut mixture among the pans and spread it into an even layer. Divide the sweet potato filling among the pans and smooth the surface. Top each pie with a few pecan halves. Bake for about 50 to 60 minutes, or until golden.

*Makes 8 servings.*

# Miniature Pecan Pies

Barbara Cameron got her start managing talent in the entertainment industry in her own home by having two talented children. She now has moved on to owning a successful Hollywood talent agency. When everyone is home for the holidays, these pies are a family favorite, served as tiny bonuses with coffee and tea at dessert time.

### PASTRY

| | |
|---|---|
| ½ | cup margarine, at room temperature |
| 1 | package (3 ounces) cream cheese, at room temperature |
| 1 | cup all-purpose flour |

### FILLING

| | |
|---|---|
| ¾ | cup firmly packed brown sugar |
| 1 | large egg |
| 1 | tablespoon margarine, melted |
| 1 | teaspoon vanilla extract |
| | Dash of salt |
| ⅔ | cup coarsely broken pecans |

▪ *To make the pastry:* In a large bowl, using an electric mixer, cream the margarine and cream cheese thoroughly. Beat in the flour until well blended. Wrap the dough in plastic and refrigerate overnight.

▪ Preheat the oven to 325° F.

▪ Butter the cups of a 24-cup miniature muffin tin. Divide the dough into 24 balls and press each ball into the prepared muffin cups.

▪ *To make the filling:* In a medium bowl, mix together the brown sugar, egg, margarine, vanilla, and salt until blended. Stir in the pecans.

▪ Spoon the mixture into the pastry-lined cups. Bake for about 25 minutes, or until the crust is lightly browned. Cool in the pan on a wire rack.

*Makes 24 miniature pies.*

# CHRISTMAS CHEESECAKE

This Christmassy dessert is Craig Claiborne's interpretation of a recipe that was demonstrated to him nearly 20 years ago by a chef at the restaurant adjoining the ice-skating rink in New York City's Rockefeller Center. Craig recommends serving the cheesecake with a dry white wine or a sweeter wine such as a sauterne or gewürztraminer. To add an extra-special touch, garnish the top of the cake with candied fruit that has been cut into shapes.

| | |
|---|---|
| About ⅓ | *cup graham cracker crumbs* |
| ½ | *pound candied fruit, such as citrus, cherries, watermelon rind* |
| 2 | *pounds cream cheese, at room temperature* |
| ½ | *cup heavy cream* |
| 4 | *large eggs* |
| 1¾ | *cups granulated sugar* |
| 1 | *teaspoon vanilla extract* |

▪ Preheat the oven to 300° F.

▪ Butter the inside of a metal cake pan that is 8 inches wide and 3 inches deep. (Do *not* use a springform pan.) Sprinkle the inside with graham cracker crumbs. Shake out the excess crumbs and set the pan aside.

*Barbara Cameron is used to cooking with celebrities—her son, Kirk Cameron, plays Mike Seaver on "Growing Pains," and her daughter, Candace Cameron, plays D.J. in "Full House."*

▪ Cut the candied fruit into pieces that are ¼ inch or smaller.

▪ To make the cheesecake mixture, you can use either a food processor or an electric mixer. (The processor is faster.) Place the cream cheese, cream, eggs, sugar, and vanilla in the container of a food processor fitted with a metal chopping blade or in the bowl of an electric mixer. If you are using a processor, blend the ingredients thoroughly. If you are using a mixer, start beating the ingredients on low and as the ingredients blend, increase the speed to high. Add the pieces of candied fruit and stir to blend.

▪ Pour and scrape the batter into the prepared pan. Shake the pan gently to level the mixture.

▪ Place the pan inside a larger baking pan and add enough boiling water so that it comes about ½ inch up the side of the inner pan. (This is a water bath.) Do not let the edge of the cheesecake pan touch the sides of the larger pan. Set the pans in the oven and bake for 2 hours. At the end of that time, turn off the oven heat and let the cake remain in the oven for 1 hour longer.

■ Lift the cake pan out of its water bath and place it on a rack. Let stand for at least 2 hours.

■ To unmold the cheesecake, place a round cake plate over the cake pan and carefully turn both upside down. Serve the cheesecake lukewarm or at room temperature.

*Makes 12 servings.*

# CHRISTMAS TIRAMISU

Marcello Russodivito, chef and owner of Marcello's in Suffern, New York, presented his easy recipe for a very special Italian dessert. *Tiramisu* means "pick-me-up"—and this is an ideal dish to make when you are caught up in the frenzy of the holiday season. Marcello (now 30-something) started his culinary career at the age of 12 in a restaurant near Rome and he's been expanding his repertoire of recipes ever since.

Serve this layered dessert in a pretty glass or ceramic dish. Leftovers are equally delicious the next day. Use any sweet wine such as port, Madeira, or a sweet white wine. Mascarpone is an Italian cheese that is similar to a rich cream cheese. It can usually be found in gourmet stores, Italian markets, or in the cheese section of some supermarkets.

Note: Use a serrated knife to cut the angel-food or sponge cake into ½–inch-thick slices, using a sawing motion. If it is too difficult to dip the cake slices into the coffee, place the cake in the dish instead and spoon the coffee over the cake.

| | |
|---|---|
| 1 | *pound mascarpone or cream cheese, softened* |
| ³⁄₄ | *cup granulated sugar* |
| 8 | *large egg yolks* |
| ½ | *cup sweet wine* |
| About 2 | *cups espresso or very strong black coffee* |
| About 9 | *ounces of ladyfingers or 14 ounces of angel-food cake or sponge cake, thinly sliced* |
| 1 | *tablespoon unsweetened cocoa powder* |

▪ In a small bowl, using a fork, beat the cheese until creamy. Set aside.

▪ Place a large (about 10- to 12-cup capacity) metal bowl over a pot of boiling water. Using a hand-held electric mixer set on medium-high, beat the sugar and egg yolks in the bowl for 1 minute, or until the mixture is well blended. With the mixer set on low speed (to prevent splashing), gradually add the wine. Continue to cook and beat the mixture, increasing the speed to medium and then to high as the mixture thickens. Cook and beat for 5 to 7 minutes, or until the mixture is thickened and light, scraping down the sides of the bowl frequently with a rubber spatula.

▪ Remove the bowl from the heat and continue to beat the mixture for 1 minute longer. Beat in the cheese just until blended (makes about 5 cups).

▪ Pour 1 cup of the espresso into a small shallow bowl that is large enough to hold a ladyfinger if it is placed horizontally in the bowl.

▪ Quickly dip the rounded top side of each ladyfinger into the espresso. Only the top half of the ladyfingers should be soaked with espresso. (If the ladyfingers get too wet, they will fall apart.) Add more coffee to the bowl as needed.

▪ Place the ladyfingers, flat side down, in the bottom of a 13-by-9-inch glass or ceramic dish to form a single layer. (Do not use a metal pan.) Pour half of the custard mixture over the ladyfingers and spread to cover them. Dip the remaining ladyfingers in espresso (there will be a few extra ladyfingers) and form a second layer over the custard mixture. Pour the remaining custard mixture over the ladyfingers and spread to an even layer.

▪ Place the cocoa powder in a strainer and dust the top of the tiramisu evenly with the cocoa powder. Cover and refrigerate for at least 10 hours.

*Makes 10 to 12 servings.*

## WHAT IS YOUR MOST UNUSUAL DINNERTIME MEMORY?

**KATHIE LEE:** My mom is great, but she likes to throw things when she gets mad. And she would often get mad at dinnertime. So it was not unusual for a piece of chicken to go flying past you. Or maybe a pork chop would put your eye out if you weren't careful. Somehow most of the food found its way into our stomachs!

*Family Favorites*

*Kathie Lee and substitute co-host Frank Gifford share a smile.*

# KATHIE LEE'S SAUSAGE AND SAGE THANKSGIVING STUFFING

Kathie Lee took a turn in the kitchen and prepared her extra-special recipe for stuffing. It's much too good to save just for Thanksgiving, though. Remember, once you get a turkey in the oven, the rest is plain sailing—*and* you get great leftovers! This recipe can easily be cut in half.

| | |
|---|---|
| ½ | *cup (1 stick) butter* |
| 8 | *celery ribs, chopped* |
| 1 | *large onion, peeled and chopped* |
| 2 | *pounds pork sausage* |
| 2 | *packages (16 ounces each) herb-seasoned stuffing* |
| | *Ground sage to taste* |
| | *Salt and pepper to taste* |

*(Steve Friedman/Buena Vista Television)*

▪ In a large saucepan, heat the butter over medium-high heat. Cook the celery and onion for 10 to 15 minutes, or until the vegetables are softened.

▪ In a large skillet, cook the sausage over medium-high heat until cooked through. Drain the fat from the meat and discard.

▪ In a large bowl, combine the vegetable mixture, cooked sausage, and bread croutons. Add a little water to moisten the stuffing slightly. Season with sage, salt, and pepper. Use to stuff a turkey. Bake any leftover stuffing in a buttered baking dish.

*Makes enough to stuff a 20-pound turkey.*

# KATHIE LEE'S SPECIAL TURKEY MARSALA

Kathie Lee loves the lemony taste of this simple recipe she got from her mother, Joan Epstein, who originally made the recipe with veal, but adapted it later for use with turkey. You can use fresh garlic instead of the garlic salt if you like. Marsala is a sweet and highly prized wine from Sicily.

| | |
|---|---|
| ¹⁄₂ | *cup all-purpose flour* |
| ¹⁄₄ | *cup grated Parmesan cheese* |
| 1 | *pound of ¹⁄₄-inch-thick turkey cutlets* |
| | *Salt, pepper, and paprika to taste* |
| 2 | *tablespoons butter* |
| 2 | *tablespoons olive oil* |
| | *Garlic salt to taste* |
| ¹⁄₂ to ³⁄₄ | *cup marsala wine* |
| 2 | *tablespoons fresh lemon juice* |
| | *Lemon wedges, for garnish* |

- In a shallow dish, mix the flour and cheese.

- Sprinkle the turkey cutlets with salt, pepper, and paprika. Dip the cutlets in the flour mixture to lightly coat both sides; shake off any excess.

- In a large skillet, heat the butter and olive oil over medium heat until the butter is melted. Lightly sprinkle the pan with garlic salt.

- Cook the cutlets for 30 to 60 seconds on each side until they are lightly browned. Stir in the marsala and lemon juice. Simmer for about 3 minutes, or just until the turkey is cooked through.

- Arrange the cutlets on a warm serving platter and pour the remaining liquid in the skillet over the cutlets. Garnish with lemon wedges.

*Makes 4 servings.*

# $M$ICHIE'S SWEET POTATO "SOUFFLÉ"

Michie Mader is Kathie Lee's sister and a talented singer, who often serves as a backup vocalist for Kathie Lee and Regis. She appeared on "Live" with her daughter, Shannie, just before Thanksgiving in 1989. Thanksgiving is the official start to the holiday season at their home, and this recipe is a family favorite especially beloved by Kathie Lee. The recipe was given to their family by Genevieve Johnson, and both Kathie Lee and Michie swear that even those who do not love sweet potatoes will like this dish!

|         |                                                          |
|---------|----------------------------------------------------------|
| 3       | *pounds sweet potatoes or yams, peeled and cut into cubes* |
| 2       | *large eggs*                                             |
| ³/₄     | *cup firmly packed brown sugar, divided*                 |
| ½       | *cup (1 stick) butter, melted and divided*               |
| 1       | *teaspoon salt*                                          |
| 1       | *teaspoon ground cinnamon*                               |
| Up to ½ | *cup orange juice*                                       |
| 1       | *cup pecan halves*                                       |

- Preheat the oven to 375° F.

- In a large saucepan over high heat, bring the potatoes and enough water to cover them to a boil. Reduce the heat, cover, and simmer for 15 to 20 minutes, or until the potatoes are soft. Drain.

- In a large bowl, beat the potatoes with an electric mixer until they are smooth. Beat in the eggs, ¼ cup of the brown sugar, ¼ cup of the butter, the salt, and cinnamon. Starting with ¼ cup, beat in just enough orange juice to make the mixture moist and fluffy.

- Scrape the sweet potato mixture into a 2- to 3-quart soufflé dish and smooth the surface into an even layer. Arrange the pecan halves over the top. Sprinkle the remaining ½ cup of brown sugar over the pecans. Drizzle the top with the remaining ¼ cup of melted butter.

- Bake for 25 to 30 minutes, or until the top is bubbly all over.

*Makes 8 to 10 servings.*

# $K$*RINGA* (S*WEDISH* P*UFF*)

Joan Epstein, Kathie Lee's mother, gave a "command performance" on "Live" just before Christmas 1991. This recipe was given to Joan 27 years ago by her Swedish friend, Nyona Erickson, and ever since, almond-flavored Kringa has been a favorite Christmas tradition in the Epstein family. If you like, you can add a pinch of salt to the crust and puff portions of the recipe.

CRUST

| | |
|---|---|
| 1 | *cup all-purpose flour* |
| ½ | *cup (1 stick) unsalted chilled butter, cut into ½-inch cubes* |
| 2 | *tablespoons ice water, divided* |

## PUFF

| | |
|---|---|
| 1 | cup water |
| ½ | cup (1 stick) unsalted butter, cut into ½-inch cubes |
| 1 | cup all-purpose flour |
| 3 | extra-large eggs |
| ½ | teaspoon almond extract or vanilla extract |

## BUTTERCREAM ICING

| | |
|---|---|
| 1 | cup (2 sticks) unsalted butter |
| 4 | cups confectioners' sugar |
| 2 | tablespoons milk, divided |
| 1 | teaspoon vanilla extract |

▪ *To make the crust:* Place the flour and butter in a large bowl. Using a pastry blender, 2 knives used scissors-fashion, or your fingertips, work the butter into the flour until the pieces of butter are no larger than peas. Sprinkle 1 tablespoon of the ice water over the flour mixture and stir with a fork until it begins to hold together. Press the dough into a ball. (If the dough remains dry and crumbly, sprinkle the remaining 1 tablespoon of water over the dough and stir until it holds together.) Divide the dough in half and wrap both pieces in plastic. Refrigerate for about 1 hour, or until firm.

▪ Remove the dough from the refrigerator. Lightly dust one piece of the dough with flour and, using your fingers, pat it into the shape of a rectangle. Place the dough between 2 sheets of waxed paper and roll the dough into a strip that measures about 13 by 4 inches. Peel off the top piece of waxed paper. Invert the dough onto a 15½-by-10½-inch jelly-roll pan, leaving room beside it for the second piece of dough. Peel off the second piece of waxed paper. (If the waxed paper is difficult to remove, chill the dough on the jellyroll pan until the dough is firm, then, very gently, peel off the waxed paper.) Trim the edges of the dough so that they are straight. Repeat with the second piece of dough. Refrigerate the pan of dough while you make the puff.

▪ *To make the puff:* Preheat the oven to 375° F. In a medium saucepan, combine the water and the butter. Cook over medium heat until the butter is melted. Increase the heat to medium-high and bring the water and butter to a boil. Remove the pan from the heat. Stir in the flour and continue stirring vigorously until the batter is smooth.

▪ Transfer the dough to a large bowl. One at a time, beat in the eggs, beating well after each addition. Stir in the vanilla or almond extract.

▪ Remove the pan of dough from the refrigerator. Spread half of the puff mixture in an even layer over one of the strips. Spread the remaining puff mixture over the second strip. Bake for 35 to 40 minutes, or until golden brown. The puff layer should be dry and firm.

▪ Set the pan on a wire rack and cool the pastries completely.

▪ *To make the buttercream:* In a large bowl, beat the butter until smooth. Gradually add the confectioners' sugar and continue beating on medium-high until smooth. Add enough milk to make the buttercream a creamy, spreadable consistency. Beat in the vanilla or almond extract.

▪ Divide the buttercream in half and spread in an even layer over the top of each cooled pastry. Slice each pastry diagonally into 10 slices.

*Makes 20 servings.*

Steve Friedman/Buena Vista Television

*Regis and Executive Producer Michael Gelman get acquainted with the audience.*

# JALAPEÑO CASSEROLE

With recipes like this one from his mother, Rhoda Gelman, it's no wonder executive producer Michael Gelman appreciates good cooking! Rhoda Gelman has taken many cooking classes and taught a class herself, "Gourmet Cooking for Kids." She cooks frequently for friends and business associates and has catered numerous functions.

You could serve this casserole for brunch or as a simple, homey supper dish. If you like, substitute cooked, crumbled sausage for some, or all of the cheese. A seasonal fresh fruit salad would be a nice accompaniment.

|   |   |
|---|---|
| 1 | *can (7 ounces) green chilies, with seeds removed, drained* |
| 3 | *cups shredded Monterey jack and/or cheddar cheese* |
| 2 | *medium tomatoes, peeled and sliced* |
| 4 | *large eggs* |
| 1½ | *cups evaporated milk* |
| ¾ | *cup all-purpose flour* |
| 1 | *teaspoon salt* |
|   | *Sliced avocado and sour cream, for garnish* |

▪ Preheat the oven to 350° F. Lightly butter an 11-by-7-inch glass baking dish.

▪ Arrange the chilies on the bottom of the casserole. Top with an even layer of the cheese and then the sliced tomatoes.

▪ In a large bowl, whisk the eggs until they are frothy. Gradually whisk in the evaporated milk, flour, and salt. Carefully pour the egg mixture over the layers in the dish. Bake 50 to 60 minutes, or until lightly browned. Serve in squares garnished with avocado slices and sour cream.

*Makes 6 servings.*

## WHAT ARE YOUR FAVORITE FAMILY RECIPES?

**REGIS:** "Joy's chicken—and she makes great Italian dishes. In my family, we had great celebrations at Thanksgiving and Christmas with a turkey. I also especially remember my mother's ham and lasagna."

**KATHIE LEE:** "My mom could *write* a cookbook! She learned to cook on her own. Our family likes spaghetti, lasagna, and sausage stuffing at Thanksgiving."

# GELMAN'S CHICKEN AMORE

On the production sheet, this segment was called "Gelmonster Gastronomics." Executive Producer Michael Gelman prepared this seductive recipe as the grand finale of a week of bachelor cooking. In addition to decorating the kitchen, lowering the lights, and playing Ravel's "Bolero," Michael and Regis sported satin smoking jackets. At the end of the segment, Gelman was surprised by three women in bikinis who covered him with kisses.

| | |
|---|---|
| 4 | boneless chicken breasts (with or without skin) |
| 1 | cup all-purpose flour |
| | Salt and pepper to taste |
| ½ | cup "extra" extra-virgin olive oil |
| 1 | cup dry white wine |
| ¼ | cup chopped fresh parsley |
| 2 | garlic cloves, mashed |
| ½ | teaspoon poultry seasoning |
| | Dash of Tabasco |
| ¾ | cup pitted and sliced ripe olives |
| 1 | cup sliced fresh or canned mushrooms |
| 1 | jar (7 ounces) pimientos or roasted red peppers, drained and cut into ¼-inch strips |
| | Freshly cooked buttered noodles |

- In a shallow dish, mix the flour, salt, and pepper. Dip the chicken in the flour mixture to lightly coat; shake off any excess.

- In a large skillet, heat the oil over medium heat. Cook the chicken breasts for 3 to 5 minutes on each side until they are lightly browned.

- In a small bowl, stir together the wine, parsley, garlic, poultry seasoning, salt, pepper, and Tabasco. Pour this over the chicken. Scatter the olives, mushrooms, and pimientos over the chicken. Cover the skillet and simmer for about 35 minutes, or until cooked through. Serve over buttered noodles.

*Makes 4 servings.*

# JOY'S PASTA WITH CHICKEN AND BROCCOLI

Regis raved about this dish on "Live" one day, and shortly afterward, his wife Joy demonstrated the recipe on the show. Michael Gelman has renamed this dish "Pasta à la Passion."

| | |
|---|---|
| ¼ | cup extra-virgin olive oil |
| 2 | garlic cloves, finely chopped |
| ½ | pound boneless, skinless chicken breasts, cut into ½-inch-wide strips |
| 1½ | cups small broccoli florets |
| ¾ | cup oil-packed sun-dried tomatoes, drained and sliced thin |
| 1 | teaspoon dried basil leaves |
| | Pinch crushed red pepper flakes |
| | Salt and pepper to taste |
| ¼ | cup dry white wine |
| ¾ | cup chicken broth |
| 1 | tablespoon butter or margarine |
| ½ | pound bow-tie pasta, cooked according to package directions and drained |
| | Grated Parmesan cheese (optional) |

▪ In a large skillet, heat the oil over medium heat.

▪ Sauté the garlic for about 1 minute, until golden, stirring constantly. Add the chicken strips and sauté until white and almost completely cooked. Add the broccoli and sauté until crisply tender, then add the sun-dried tomatoes, red pepper flakes, salt, and pepper. Add the wine, then the broth and butter and cook for about 3 to 5 minutes, or until heated through, stirring occasionally.

▪ Toss the cooked pasta with the chicken mixture. Serve with Parmesan cheese, if desired.

*Makes 4 servings.*

# RESOURCES

———■□■———

"LIVE with Regis & Kathie Lee" mugs and t-shirts are available from:

LIVE Merchandise
c/o "LIVE with Regis & Kathie Lee"
P.O. Box 450329
El Paso, TX 88545-0329

To write to Regis and Kathie Lee:

Regis Philbin and/or Kathie Lee Gifford
"LIVE with Regis & Kathie Lee"
7 Lincoln Square
5th Floor
New York, NY 10023

For tickets to see "LIVE":

"LIVE" Tickets
Ansonia Station
P.O. Box 777
New York, NY 10023-0777

To enter "LIVE's" Trivia Contest:

"LIVE" Trivia Contest
Ansonia Station
P.O. Box 108
New York, NY 10023

To get "LIVE's" newsletter ($1.00 plus a self-addressed, stamped envelope):

"LIVE with Regis & Kathie Lee" Newsletter
Issue #
P.O. Box 2010
Floral Park, NY 11002

*INGREDIENTS*

For Mexican ingredients, write to:

Jane Butel's Pecos Valley Spice Co.
4371 Charlotte Highway
3 Heritage Park
Lake Wylie, SC 29710
803-831-0121

For Helen's Jamaican Jerk (ready-to-use marinade and rub), contact:

Helen's Tropical-Exotics
3519 Church Street
Clarkston, GA 30021
1-800-544-JERK

For persimmon pulp, contact:

Dillman Farm
4955 West State Road 45
Bloomington, IN 47403
812-825-5525

For MAGIC Seasoning Blends™ by Chef Paul Prudhomme, check major supermarkets or contact:

MAGIC Seasoning Blends™
P.O. Box 23342
New Orleans, LA 70183-0342
800-457-2857

For The Clever Cleaver Brothers' cookbook and videotapes, write to:

Clever Cleaver Productions
968 Emerald Street, Suite 51
San Diego, CA 92109

For the Love Chef's cookbook, videotapes, and recipe computer software, write to:

Cooking With Love
210 Fifth Avenue
New York, NY 10010

For the *First Gentleman's Cookbook*, contact:

First Gentleman's Cookbook
Governor's Mansion
Lincoln, NE 68508

## COOKBOOKS

Francis Anthony. *Cooking With Love: The Love Chef Shows You How*. Henry Holt & Co. 1990.

Rose Levy Beranbaum. *The Cake Bible*. William Morrow and Company, Inc. 1988.

Jane Brody. *Jane Brody's Good Food Gourmet: Menus & Recipes for Delicious & Healthful Entertaining*. Norton. 1990.

Jane Butel. *Hotter Than Hell*. HP Books. 1987.

Stephen J. Cassarino and Lee N. Gerovitz. *Cookin' With The Cleavers*. Wynwood Press. 1990.

Craig Claiborne. *The Revised New York Times Cookbook*. Harper Collins. 1990.

Annemarie Colbin. *The Natural Gourmet*. Ballantine Books. 1989.

*Betty Crocker's Cookbook, 40th Anniversary Edition*. By General Mills, Inc. Minneapolis, Minn. 1991, 1986, 1978, 1969. Prentice Hall General Reference, a division of Simon & Schuster.

Marion Cunningham. *Fanny Farmer Cookbook* (revised 13th edition). Alfred A. Knopf, Inc. 1990.

Marcel Desaulniers. *The Trellis Cookbook: Contemporary American Cooking in Williamsburg*. Fireside/Simon & Schuster. 1992.

Merle Ellis. *Cutting Up in the Kitchen*. Chronicle Books. 1975.

Dean Fearing. *Dean Fearing's Southwest Cuisine: Blending Asia and the Americas*. Grove Weidenfeld. 1990.

Joyce Goldstein. *The Mediterranean Kitchen*. William Morrow and Company, Inc. 1989.

Laurie Burrows Grad. *Make It Easy, Make It Light*. Simon & Schuster. 1987.

Fred and Linda Griffith. *The Best of the Midwest*. Viking Studio Books. 1990.

Madhur Jaffrey. *A Taste of India*. Atheneum. 1988.

Phyllis C. Kaufman. *The Good Eating, Good Health Cookbook*. Consumer Reports Books. 1990.

Jenifer Lang. *Jenifer Lang Cooks for Kids*. Harmony. 1991.

Robin Leach. *The Lifestyles of the Rich & Famous Cookbook*. Viking Penguin USA. 1992.

Ismail Merchant. *Ismail Merchant's Indian Cuisine*. A Fireside Book by Simon & Schuster. 1986.

The Moosewood Collective. *Sundays at Moosewood Restaurant*. Vegetable Kingdom, Inc. Simon & Schuster. 1990.

William D. Orr. *First Gentleman's Cookbook*. Jacob North Printing Company, Inc. 1989.

Jean-Louis Palladin. *Jean-Louis: Cooking With the Seasons*. Thomasson-Grant. 1989.

Francine Prince. *Francine Prince's New Jewish Cuisine*. G.P. Putnam's Sons/ Perigee Books. 1991.

Paul Prudhomme. *Chef Paul Prudhomme's Seasoned America*. William Morrow and Company, Inc. 1991.

Paul Prudhomme. *The Prudhomme Family Cookbook*. William Morrow and Company, Inc. 1987.

Paul Prudhomme. *Chef Paul Prudhomme's Louisiana Kitchen*. William Morrow and Company, Inc. 1984.

Joanna Pruess. *Supermarket Epicure: Great Recipes & Smart Shopping for Today's Lifestyle*. William Morrow/Quill. 1988.

Joel Rapp. *Fabulous Fish*. A Fawcett Columbine Book, published by Ballantine Books. 1991.

Michael Roberts. *Fresh From the Freezer*. Morrow. 1990.

Michael Roberts. *Secret Ingredients*. Bantam. 1988.

Phillip Stephen Schulz. *As American as Apple Pie*. Simon & Schuster. 1990.

Tommy Tang. *Modern Thai Cuisine*. Doubleday. 1991.

Lynne Tolley and Pat Mitchamore. *Jack Daniel's Hometown Celebration Cookbook*. Rutledge Hill Press. 1990.

Lynne Tolley and Pat Mitchamore. *Jack Daniel's The Spirit of Tennessee Cookbook*. Rutledge Hill Press. 1988.

Jennifer Trainer and Elizabeth Wheeler. *The Yachting Cookbook*. Random House/Crown. 1990.

Carole Walter. *Great Cakes*. Ballantine Books, Inc. 1991.

Mary Ward and Carol Stine. *Blue Ribbon Breads*. 1989.

Mary Ward. *The Hodgson Mill Oat Bran Cookbook and Guide to Reducing Blood Cholesterol*. 1988.

Janos Wilder. *Janos: Recipes and Tales From a Southwest Restaurant*. Ten Speed Press. 1989.

Helen Willinsky. *Barbecue From Jamaica*. The Crossing Press. 1990.

# INDEX

## A

Ackerman, Roy, 76
Albrecht, Paul, 101
Albright, Barbara, 166, 195, 207
Ambrose, Anthony, 171
Andouille, shrimp Samantha with, 113
Angel-hair pasta cacio e Pepe, 46–47
Anthony, Francis (the Love Chef), 3, 7, 13, 21,
    42, 44, 45, 82, 97, 121, 142, 163, 165,
    182, 193, 220, 221, 222, 223
Aoki, Rocky, 175
Appetizers. *See* Starters
Apple butter, pork chops stuffed with, 72–73
Apple cake, German, 195–195
Apple Napoleon, spiced, 171
Apples, saffron, with frozen pistachio yogurt,
    172–173
Arnold, Sam'l P., 22
Auden, Bruce, 172
Avocado sauce, salmon with, 126–127

## B

Banana pudding, homemade, 193–194
Barbecue sauces and marinades
    Jack Daniel's rib glaze, 66
    Jamaican jerk rub, 106–107
    ribs Excalibur, 67–68
    tequila-lime, 134–135
    traditional, steak, 54–55
Barbecue tips, 108
Battistini, Stefano, 216
Beans, Riverbank barbecue baked, 145
Beef. *See also* Steak
    burgers, 63
    how to age, 53
    meatballs, 59
    meatloaf, 61, 62
    pot roast, 64–65
    tacos, 60
    Texas-style skillet, 177
Beer batter fish and spicy dipping sauce, 130
Bell, Lola Yvonne, 89, 115, 135
Beranbaum, Rose Levy, 199
Berkowitz, Roger, 23
Beverages
    Christmas punch. 221–222
    the polar breeze, 222–223

Bing cherry crumb cake, 157–158
Blueberries
    about, 162
    muffins, 161–162
Boulor, Philippe, 79
Bowtie pasta
    bat-wing, 37–38
    Joy's pasta with chicken and broccoli, 243–
        244
    à la marcello, 43
Bread(s)
    Irish freckle, 153–154
    spoon, 143
    traditional Italian, 152–153
Bread pudding, Georgia peach, 192
Broccoli
    Joy's pasta with chicken and, 243–244
    pan-seared salmon with zucchini, spinach,
        and, 127–128
    pasta with mushrooms and, 44
Brody, Jane, 28
Brody, Lora, 150
Brownies, low-cal, 183
Buffalo chicken wings, 7
Burgers, Rusty-, 63
Butel, Jane, 56
Butter(s)
    apple, 72–73
    guacamole, 5

## C

Cake(s)
    bing cherry crumb, 157–158
    carrot, Joseph's knockout, 205–206
    the chocolate denseness, 195–197
    chocolate oblivion truffle torte, 199–200
    German apple, 194–195
    pan de Jerez (chocolate sherry torte), 201–202
    pecan pound, Aunt Pittypat's, 203–204
Cameron, Barbara, 227
Campion, Elma, 124
Carrot cake, Joseph's knockout, 205–206
Cassarino, Steve. *See* Clever Cleaver Brothers
Casserole, jalapeño, 241–242
Cheese
    balls, 15

Cheese (cont'd.)
  spread, 15
  Swiss, fondue, 6
Cheesecake(s)
  Christmas, 228–230
  white chocolate, 198–199
Chef Tell. *See* Erhardt, Tell
Chicken
  barbecued, prehistoric, 107–108
  Bastille day, 92
  breast, baked in pastry, 101–102
  breast, bundle of love, 93
  breast, with garden vegetables, 96–97
  breast, Gelman's chicken amore, 242–243
  breast, grilled with watermelon pico de gallo, 104–105
  breast, Jamaican jerk rub, 106–107
  breast, Joy's pasta with broccoli and, 243–244
  breast, marinated, for pasta salad, 40
  breast, pick-up sticks, 109
  breast, with prosciutto and cheese with mushroom sauce, 94–95
  breast, stuffed with guacamole butter, 5
  Buffalo chicken wings, 7
  Caribbean-fried, 89–90
  with fruit, 105–106
  Gaeltach, 217–218
  kebabs, 109
  marinade for, 55
  matzoh balls with, 99–100
  Moghlai, 87–88
  nuggets, nautical, 8
  pan-fried, Southwestern, 98–99
  pilaf, 97
  roasted chili, 90–91
  soup, bowl of the wife of Kit Carson, 22
  soup, sensational, 20
  tacos, 60
  Texas-style skillet, 177
  Tucson, 176
  yogurt, 88–89
Chili, Super Bowl, 25–26
Chocolate
  brownies, low-cal, 183
  cheesecake, white, 198–199
  cookies, turtle, 207–208
  the chocolate denseness (cake), 195–197
  fudge, million-dollar, 210–211
  how to melt, 197
  love bites, 182
  pan de Jerez (chocolate sherry torte), 201–202
  pie, pecan, 187–188
  pie, whipped cream, 188–189
  sauce, 196
  truffle torte, chocolate oblivion, 199–200
  waffles, cocoa, 167–168
Ciao, Johnny, 136
Claiborne, Craig, 187, 228

Clam chowder, New England, 23
Clever Cleaver Brothers, 19, 54, 59, 70, 72, 107, 108, 148, 218
Cod, lemon crumb-baked, 121
Colbin, Annemarie, 29
Cookies
  chocolate turtle, 207–208
  merveilles, 208–209
Copeland, Marcia, 64
Corn
  bread. *See* Spoon bread
  on the cob, perfect, 146–147
  fritters, 147
Crawfish, shrimp, or crabmeat in cream sauce, pasta in, 36–37
Crêpes, easy French, 164
Cucumber sauce, Irish salmon in, 124–125

D
Dano, Linda, 41
Darren, James, 47
Davis, Rich, 109
Desaulniers, Marcel, 127
Dessert(s). *See also* Brownies; Cakes; Cheesecakes; Chocolate; Cookies; Pies; Puddings; Tortes
  chocolate brownies, low-cal, 183
  chocolate love bites, 182
  Christmas tiramisu, 230–231
  fighting Irish flambé, 218–219
  kringa (Swedish puff), 238–240
  million-dollar fudge, 210–211
  New Year's trifle, 215
  persimmon and maple fool, 176
  saffron apples with frozen pistachio yogurt, 172–173
  spiced apple napoleon, 171
Dessert sauces
  chocolate, 196
  raspberry, 198
Dickerson, Helen, 144
Diller, Phyllis, 27
Dingeldein, Russell, 188
Doran, Eamonn, 217

E
Eggplant pie, Robin Leach's Mediterranean, 12–13
Egg rolls, vegetable, 10–11
Eggs
  stuffed, 15, 16
  hard-cooked, how to make, 15
Ellis, Merle, 52, 53
Epstein, Joan, 238
Erhardt, Tell (Chef Tell), 14, 40, 69, 83, 138, 146, 147, 166, 189, 194, 198, 224

F
Fajitas, flaming, 56–57
Farfalle. *See* Bowtie pasta

Fearing, Dean, 104
Fettuccine with broccoli and mushrooms, 44
Fish. *See also* Shellfish; *specific types of fish and shellfish*
    beer batter, and spicy dipping sauce, 131–132
    cod, lemon crumb-baked, 121
    nuggets, nautical, 9
    with puff sauce, 130–131
    salmon, 124–128, 133
    Santa Barbara surfer's saute, 136–137
    seafood kebabs, 134–135
    seafood salad, seasoned rice, 122–123
    snapper, 135–136, 138
    tuna salad, warm, 129
Flay, Bobby, 90, 141
Flambé, fighting Irish, 218–219
Fondue, Swiss cheese, 6
Fowl. *See* Chicken; Turkey
Frittata, sweetheart, 165
Frobuccino, Marilyn, 149
Fruit, chicken with, 105–106
Fudge, million-dollar, 210–211
Fullmer, Earl "Butch," 130


G
Gelman, Michael, 242
Gelman, Rhoda, 241
George, Peter, 174
Gerin, Jean-Louis, 92
Gerovitz, Lee. *See* Clever Cleaver Brothers
Gifford, Kathie Lee, 235, 236
Gillett, Eric Michael, 71
Goebel, Stephen, 33
Gold, Rozanne, 20
Goldstein, Joyce, 201
Goose, roast Christmas, 224
Gowdy, Curt, 144
Grad, Laurie Burrows, 34
Green peppercorn sauce, pork tenderloin medallions with, 70
Griffith, Fred, 159
Guacamole, Hard Rock, 4–5
Guerithault, Vincent, 114


H
Ham
    cornets, 14
    Kentucky Christmas, 223
    rolls, 14
    spread, spicy, 14
Hartley, Sandy, 93
Hors d'oeuvres, 14–16


I
Irish freckle bread, 153–154
Italian bread, traditional, 152–153

J
Jalapeño casserole, 241
Jamaican jerk rub, 106–107

K
Kaufman, Peter, 62
Kaufman, Phyllis, 161
Kebab(s)
    chicken pick-up sticks, 109
    seafood, 134–135
    tips for making, 108
Klaskala, Gerry, 192
Kringa (Swedish puff), 238–240

L
Lamb
    chops with cracked pepper and tarragon, 75–76
    chops in parmesan crust, 74–75
    Easter roast leg of, with scallions and potatoes, 216–217
    marinade for, 55
    navarin of, 70
    paprikas, 78
    shepherd's pie, 76–77
Lang, Jenifer, 10
Latkes, potato, 180–181
Leach, Robin, 12
Leftovers
    cheese, for hors d'oeuvres, 15
    Chinese food, for egg rolls, 11
    guacamole, 5
    lamb, 76
    steak, 51
    turkey, 102
Lentil, red, hearty lemon soup, 29–30
Lettuce soup, 19
Lime pie, island, 189–190
Linguine
    with broccoli and mushrooms, 44
    with sweet/sauce, 34–35
Love Chef, the. *See* Anthony, Francis

M
Macgregor, Beany, 4, 5
Mader, Michie, 237
Madhur, Jaffrey, 87
Magliulo, Luciano, 96
Manetti, Larry, 51
Maple and persimmon fool, 176
Marinades. *See* Barbecue sauces and marinades
Martin, Pol, 58, 118
Matzoh balls with chicken, 99–100
Mayonnaise, guacamole, 5
Meat. *See also specific meats*
    for egg rolls, 11
Meatballs, Clever pizzaiola, 59
Meatloaf
    the governor's, 61
    Mom Kaufman's, 62

Merchant, Ismail, 88
Mezger, Kurt, 6
Milbourn, Karen, 210
Mormando, Ana Marie, 46
Muffins
    blueberry oat, 161
    honey-nut apple, 159–160
Mushrooms
    pasta with broccoli and, 44
    wild, with garlic and olive oil, 149
Mushroom sauce, chicken with prosciutto and
    cheese with, 94–95

N
Nathan, Jeffrey, 74, 94, 119, 129, 134
Noodle pudding, 150–151

O
Orr, William, 61
Oyster stew, Phyllis Diller's, 27

P
Pan de Jerez (chocolate sherry torte), 201–202
Palladin, Jean-Louis, 208
Papardelle with sausage, 33
Pasta, 33–47
    angel-hair, bucatine cacio e Pepe, 46
    bowtie, bat-wing, 37–38
    bowtie, farfalle à la Marcello, 43
    bowtie, Joy's pasta with chicken and broccoli,
        243–244
    fettuccine, with broccoli and mushrooms, 44
    how to cook, 35
    linguine with sweet red pepper sauce, 34–35
    with marinara sauce, 41
    papardelle with sausage, 33
    penne, con amore, 42
    penne, with prosciutto sauce, 45–46
    penne, Santa Fe chili, 38–39
    rigatoni, James Darren's Grandmom's, 47
    salad, party, 40–41
    spaghetti, with crawfish, shrimp, or crabmeat
        in cream sauce, 36–37
    ziti, con amore, 42
Peach bread pudding, Georgia, 192
Pecan(s)
    pie, chocolate, 187–188
    pie, holiday sweet potato, 225–227
    pies, miniature, 227–228
    pound cake, Aunt Pittypat's, 203–204
Penne pasta
    con amore, 42
    with prosciutto sauce, 45–46
    Santa Fe chili, 38
Peppers, red
    how to roast, 94
    sauce, 34–35
Perrier, Georges, 126
Persimmon and maple fool, 174

Philbin, Joy, 243
Phillips, Joseph C., 205
Piano, Pino, 102
Pick, Sam, 60
Pico de gallo, watermelon, 104
Pie(s)
    chocolate pecan, 187–188
    chocolate whipped cream, 188–189
    eggplant, Robin Leach's Mediterranean, 12–
        13
    holiday sweet potato pecan, 225–227
    island lime, 189–190
    miniature pecan, 227–228
Pilaf, chicken, 97
Pine nuts, garlic rice with, 144
Pistachio yogurt, frozen, saffron apples with,
        172–173
Pork
    chops, gypsy cutlets, 71–72
    chops, stuffed with apple butter, 72–73
    ribs, 67–68
    roast, with apricots, 69
    tenderloin medallions with green peppercorn
        sauce, 70
Potato(es)
    Easter roast leg of lamb with scallions and,
        216–217
    killer, mashed, 142
    latkes, 180–181
    salad, perfect Southwestern, 141
Pot pie, turkey, 102–103
Pot roast, classic New England, 64–65
Pound cake, Aunt Pittypat's pecan, 203–204
Prince, Francine, 99, 180
Prosciutto
    and cheese with mushroom sauce, chicken
        with, 94–95
    sauce, penne pasta with, 45–46
Prudhomme, Paul, 36, 122, 190
Pruess, Joanna, 215
Pudding(s)
    banana, homemade, 193–194
    bread, Georgia peach, 192
    Indian, Chef Paul Prudhomme's, 190–191
    noodle, 150–151

Q
Quiche, 166

R
Rapp, Joel, 131
Raspberry sauce, 198
Red peppers. See Peppers, red
Red snapper
    Lola's quick, 135–136
    snapper caprice, 138
Ribs
    barbecued, Excalibur, 67–68
    barbecued, Jack Daniel's rib glaze, 66

Rice
  garlic, with pine nuts, 144
  seasoned, seafood salad, 122–123
  thankful, 220–221
Rigatoni, James Darren's grandmom's, 47
Roberts, Michael, 75
Rotelli with crawfish, shrimp, or crabmeat in
  cream sauce, 36–37
Roussel, Michael J., 113
Russodivito, Marcello, 230

S
Salad(s)
  Clever Cleaver sweet Spring salad, 148
  grilled shrimp, with ginger, 114–115
  pasta, 40
  potato, perfect Southwestern, 141
  seasoned rice seafood, 122–123
  tuna, warm, 129
Salmon
  with avocado sauce, 126–127
  fillets with crispy skin, 133
  Irish, with cucumber sauce, 124–125
  pan-seared, with zucchini, spinach, and
    broccoli, 127–128
Salsa, Super Bowl, 3
Sammarone, Sabatino, 80
Sauces. See also Barbecue sauces and marinades;
    Dessert sauces
  avocado, 126
  hot and honey, 134–135
  marinara, 41
  pico de gallo, watermelon, 104
  prosciutto, 45–46
  puff, 130–131
  salsa, 3
  spicy dipping 131–132
  sweet red pepper, 34–35
Sausage(s)
  andouille, shrimp Samantha with, 113
  Kathie Lee's sausage and sage Thanksgiving
    stuffing, 235–236
  papardelle with, 33
Sax, Steve, 144
Scallions, Easter roast leg of lamb with potatoes
    and, 216–217
Scallops
  bay, sesame, 13
  with tomato saffron sauce, 119–120
Schiffman, Susan S., 183
Schulz, Stephen, 25
Shellfish. See also specific shellfish
  smoked oriental seafood, 120–121
Shepherd's pie, 76–77
Shish kebab. See Kebab(s)
Shrimp
  Bay State wiggle, 116–117
  ginger, 118
  grilled salad with ginger, 114

on fire, Grandma Cecilia's, 115–116
Jo Jo's juicy, 178
Samantha, with andouille, 113
and vegetables, 175
Sili, Marcello, 43
Smith, Barbara, 225
Soltner, Andre, 133
Soufflé, Michie's sweet potato, 237
Soups, 19–30
  chicken 20, 22
  clam chowder, New England, 23–24
  Easter, 20
  lettuce, 19
  oyster stew, 27
  Passover, 20
  red lentil lemon, 29–30
  split pea, 21
  vegetable, 28
Spaghetti with crawfish, shrimp, or crabmeat in
    cream sauce, 36–37
Spinach, pan-seared salmon with zucchini,
    broccoli, and, 127–128
Split pea soup, down-home, 21
Spoon bread, 143
Starters
  Buffalo chicken wings, 7
  eggplant pie, 12–13
  guacamole, 4
  hors d'oeuvres, 14–16
  nautical nuggets, 8–9
  salsa, 3
  sesame bay scallops, 13
  Swiss cheese fondue, 6
  vegetable egg rolls, 10–11
Staub, Rusty, 63
Steak(s)
  barbecue, traditional marinated, 54–55
  blackened, 52
  Diane, with cognac, 58
  fajitas, 56–57
  Lorenzo, 51
Steins, Joyce, 37
Stew(s)
  lamb, 79
  oyster, 27
Stuffing(s)
  Kathie Lee's sausage and sage, 235–236
  thankful rice, 220–221
Sugiura, Katsuo (Suki), 105
Sweet potato(es)
  holiday pecan pie, 225–227
  Michie's soufflé, 237

T
Tacos à la mayor, 60
Tang, Tommy, 38
Thicke, Alan, 153
Tiramisu, Christmas, 230–231
Tolcser, Nora, 78

Tolley, Lynne, 66, 203
Tomato saffron sauce, scallops with, 119–120
Torte(s)
    chocolate oblivion truffle, 199–200
    Pan de Jerez (chocolate sherry), 201–202
Trainer, Jennifer, 8
Trifle, New Year's, 215
Tuna salad, warm, 129
Tunks, Jeff, 120
Turkey
    marsala, Kathie Lee's special, 236
    pot pie, 102–103
    rice stuffing for, 220–221
    sausage and sage stuffing for, Kathie Lee's,
        235–236
    soup, bowl of the wife of Kit Carson, 22
Turnover, Mother's Day, 163


V
Veal
    birds, 83–84
    casino, 82
    parmigiana, 80–81
Vegetables. *See also specific vegetables*
    garden, breast of chicken with, 96–97
    egg rolls, 10–11

    shrimp and, 175
    soup, 28
Vinaigrette, guacamole, 5
Vivino, Maureen, 116
Vongerichten, Jean-Georges, 178


W
Waffles, cocoa, 167–168
Walter, Carole, 157
Ward, Mary, 152, 177
Watermelon pico de gallo, 104
White chocolate cheesecake, 198–199
Whitefish, Santa Barbara surfer's sauté, 136–137
Wilder, Janos, 98, 176
Wilk, Martin, 67
Willinsky, Helen, 106
Woesle, Martin, 164


Y
Yogurt
    chicken, 88–89
    frozen pistachio, with saffron apples, 172–173

Z
Ziti con amore, 42
Zucchini, pan-seared salmon with spinach,
    broccoli and 127–128